The Leadership
D. Roose

A Biography of the Man Whose Role Shaped American History

Anthony James Eisele

CONTENTS

1.Chief legislator

2.New Dealer

3.Second emancipator

FDR and African Americans

4.Constitutional revolutionary

FDR and the Supreme Court

5.Party leader

FDR and the Democrats

6.Communicator-in-chief

FDR's public presidency

7.Chief diplomat

FDR as foreign policy leader

8.Commander-in-chief

Structures and strategies

9.Commander-in-chief

Arsenals and alliances

10.Practical visionary

INTRODUCTION

Franklin Delano Roosevelt, one of the greatest American presidents, forged a coalition of labor, ethnic, urban, low-income, and African-American voters that fueled the Democratic Party's national ascension from the 1930s to the 1980s. During his four terms, he championed the New Deal, the greatest reform program in US history, to meet the challenges of the Great Depression, led the US to the brink of victory in WWII, and established the modern presidency as the driving force of American politics and government.

The book provided a new perspective on FDR, demonstrating how his leadership enabled the United States of America to become the most successful country of the twentieth century. This insightful and original examination of a highly consequential presidency explains how Roosevelt improved the governing capacity of his office, sparked a constitutional revolution through his interactions with the Supreme Court, and forged a new intimacy between the president and the American people through his genius for political communication. It also demonstrates the importance of his organizational and strategic leadership as commander-in-chief in America's greatest foreign war, his role in keeping the US-British-Soviet Grand Alliance together against the Axis powers, and his pioneering development of the national-security presidency that sought to promote a lasting postwar peace for the world.

1

Chief legislator

FDR and the Hundred Days

Franklin D. Roosevelt's name will be eternally linked to the New Deal program, which placed the liberal state at the center of contemporary America's growth. From March to June 1933, he presided over the most productive period of governmental activism in US history, beginning with the remarkable implementation of fifteen important laws in his first hundred days in office. No predecessor had previously pursued a legislative program of comparable magnitude for the length of his tenure, let alone at the commencement.

In his acceptance speech at the Democratic National Convention in Chicago in 1932, Roosevelt brought the term "New Deal" into the American political lexicon. In it, he pledged, 'I pledge you, I pledge myself, to a new deal for the American people.' Breaking with convention. FDR had traveled to Chicago to accept the nomination in person, rather than waiting for a party committee to bring news of his selection to the gubernatorial palace in Albany, signaling that he would not be constrained by outworn norms in the 'unique and strange times'. He had no notion that by pledging a "new deal," he was ushering in a new political era.

Though Roosevelt could see the New Deal's ultimate goal at this early point, he lacked a detailed plan to get there. On the road, there would be improvisations, blunders, and course corrections. FDR also knew that he could only move at the speed of political circumstance and popular backing.

Roosevelt was on this voyage because his prognosis of the cause of the Great Depression was diametrically opposed to Herbert Hoover's. Though not the do-nothing president of Democratic parody, the Republican incumbent relied heavily on indirect steps to promote domestic recovery. This reflected not just his dislike of statist solutions as harbingers of socialism, but also his belief that the causes of economic disaster resided outside the borders of the United States.

FDR disregarded what Rexford Tugwell called 'Hoover's argument - or excuse - that the slump had arrived "on us from abroad" as a result of war-related dislocations'. According to his interpretation, the slump was caused by internal economic and institutional flaws, most notably the misallocation of wealth, which resulted in over-saving by the wealthy and under-consumption by the rest of the country, overproduction in the farm economy, structural weaknesses in the banking system, and the reckless greed of an unregulated Wall Street.

On the campaign trail, the glaring disparities between Hoover and FDR were on display. Voters could hardly have been uninformed that if re-elected, the incumbent would abandon socioeconomic action, while the challenger planned a slew of federal initiatives to aid relief, recovery, and change. As Election Day approached, Hoover became increasingly concerned that a Roosevelt triumph would impose an alien political theory on the country. In his final big speech, he stated that "so-called new deals would destroy the very foundations of the American way of life."

Roosevelt went on to receive more popular votes (57.4%) and Electoral College votes (89%) than any other Democratic presidential candidate in history. His coattails aided congressional Democrats in achieving their largest-ever majorities in the House (313 to 117 seats) and Senate (59 to 36 seats).

Even in defeat, Hoover attempted to deflect FDR's attention away from the New Deal. In early 1933, when another wave of bank panics threatened financial collapse, Hoover requested FDR to help him in restoring public trust. On the 18th of February, he dispatched a Secret Service agent with a handwritten statement to the president-elect, in which he boasted that his policies had put the economy back on track by Election Day, only for recovery to be stalled by doubts about Roosevelt's intentions. 'I am sure,' Hoover said, 'that a very early pronouncement by you on two or three policies of your Administration will contribute considerably to restore confidence and permit the march of recovery to resume.' He advised FDR to avoid currency inflation, deficit budgets, and public projects that would overwhelm government borrowing. The outgoing president wanted his Democratic successor to agree to "the abandonment of 90% of the so-called New Deal," according to Senator David Reed (R-Pennsylvania). Unsurprisingly, FDR would oppose a treaty of surrender to a beaten foe.

When Roosevelt became office, he wasted little time in dealing with the banking crisis that Hoover had attempted to use to derail the New Deal. He urged new Treasury Secretary William Woodin on his first night in office to get an emergency bank bill ready for legislative consideration within five days. On March 5, he issued an executive order bringing Congress back into special session on March 9, and he obtained Cabinet backing for another proclamation suspending gold transactions and announcing a four-day national bank holiday.1 The bank holiday announcement had three significant effects: it bought time to frame legislation and put pressure on Congress to pass the measure quickly, it transformed the current tangle of state-mandated bank closures into a uniform approach that established federal responsibility for dealing with the crisis, and it allowed FDR to invoke patriotic unity in support of his actions.

When Roosevelt was presented with the draft measure on March 8, he met with congressional leaders from both parties that evening to win their support. The Emergency Banking Act (EBA) of 1933 granted him nearly unlimited control over bank lending, foreign exchange, and gold acquisitions. This was likely the most power given to any president in American history during peacetime. The act also empowered the Treasury to reconstruct bankrupt banks considered capable of eventually reopening their doors and authorized the Hoover-created Reconstruction Finance Corporation (RFC) to conduct capital-boosting stock purchases in these institutions, thereby expanding executive power.

When Congress reconvened on March 9, it got a stark 427-word presidential letter demanding swift passage of the bill as critical to restoring trust in the banking industry. Despite having only one printed copy, the House of Representatives adopted the resolution by voice vote after less than forty minutes of debate.

Within three days, 12,000 banks, or 70% of the country's total, had resumed operations. Long lineups formed outside the first store to open, but this time individuals were there to deposit money back into their accounts. By the end of March, $1.2 billion in money had been reintroduced into the financial system. By mid-April, another 1,300 banks had been approved to reopen, and a further 3,100 were reformed with the assistance of RFC stock purchases. Some 1,100 banks (6 percent of the total) had to be liquidated because they were unable to meet federal standards, but the EBA drafters had expected that a third of all banks would face this destiny.

Roosevelt quickly added two more victories that cemented his position as congressional leader. To reassure business and banks, EBA drafters pressed him to rebalance government finances, which had become insolvent during the Great Depression under Hoover.

To expedite matters, FDR sent a three-sentence note to Congress requesting the rapid authorization of 3.2 percent alcohol-strength beer and wine. With the country growing tired of the Prohibition experiment, a constitutional amendment repealing it, adopted by the lame-duck Congress in February, was on its way to state ratification, which was achieved in December 1933. Roosevelt's beer law resonated with Americans who were too thirsty to wait until then for a legal drink.

FDR had defeated the veterans and the dries, two of Washington's most powerful lobbies, in less than two weeks. If his first three legislative initiatives did not move America in a new direction, subsequent actions established the New Deal as a reform agenda. Consensus would be increasingly difficult to maintain in the future, even among his advisers. In his next Fireside Chat on May 7, FDR outlined his vision for federal action in the agricultural and industrial sectors

FDR began by addressing the sad state of agriculture, which employed around 21% of the nation's labor force. FDR saw the electoral need of addressing the rural situation after receiving a huge farm vote in 1932. Beyond such calculations, he had maintained throughout the 1920s that national wealth could not be sustained unless the agricultural sector shared it. By 1933, he was one of several in Washington who believed that farmers' lack of purchasing power was causing the Great Depression to last longer. Agricultural planners would eventually learn that restoring urban demand was the holistic solution to falling commodity prices. FDR would have prioritized agricultural recovery if he had known this in 1933. Despite the fact that agriculture accounted for only 8% of national economic output, significantly less than industry, banking, and services, farm interests were supported by conservative Southern Democrats who formed the backbone of party and committee leadership in Congress. As a result, putting farmers first provided the president with cover for the New Deal's unparalleled growth of the central state.

The controversial integration of agriculture into the national economy by bringing supply in line with demand and giving the federal government regulatory responsibility over production. Some farm organizations supported measures that were more in line with the agrarian ideal of self-sufficient farmers maximizing the wealth of the land.

Recognizing that the bill provided no protection for farmers facing foreclosure, Roosevelt signed an executive order on March 27 consolidating the federal government's existing rural credit agencies into the Farm Credit Administration, led by Henry Morgenthau, a neighbor and friend from the Hudson Valley. Cornell economist William Myers, Morgenthau's chief consultant, proposed a mortgage-relief proposal for inclusion in the agriculture bill. Under its parameters, $2 billion in land-bank bonds would be used to support emergency loans with a maximum interest rate of 4.5% and a five-year grace period before repayments began in order to prevent foreclosures and renegotiate existing mortgages. The volume of mortgages advanced by the new agency in 1933 was more than four times that of the entire land-bank system in 1932. The Emergency agricultural Mortgage Act, adopted as part of the omnibus agricultural bill, validated its powers, and the Farm Credit Act of 1933, signed by FDR on June 16, supplemented them. The Farm Credit Administration, one of the Hundred Days' most successful enterprises, owned roughly two-fifths of all farm-mortgage debt by 194032.

On May 12, Congress finally delivered farm measures to the president for approval, including the Agricultural Adjustment Act, the Emergency Farm Mortgage Act, and the Thomas Amendment. FDR had persuaded Senator Ellison 'Cotton Ed' Smith (D-South Carolina), an outspoken advocate of cotton production volume, to release the bill from his Senate Agriculture Committee in exchange for the appointment of his ally, George Peek, to head the Agricultural Adjustment Administration, the new agency that would administer the farm program, in a political trade. Putting a long-time opponent of production restraint in charge of the organization in charge of implementing it created complications in the future but eased the measure's passage.

Meanwhile, FDR had taken his first measures to assist the unemployed by establishing the Civilian Conservation Corps (CCC), the New Deal policy most commonly attributed to him. As governor of New York, he initiated a program that placed 10,000 jobless men to work on forestry projects. On March 9, less than a week into his presidency, Roosevelt invited the secretaries of Agriculture, Interior, and War to the White House to discuss his plan to place 500,000 unemployed men in rural camps to plant trees, protect forests, and control floods. Interior authorities were tasked with submitting a draft bill by 9.30 p.m. the same evening. This became the basis for the proposal sent to Congress on 21 March with an accompanying presidential message that the CCC would conserve forest resources, curb flooding and deliver 'moral and spiritual value' by rescuing a 'vast army' of the unemployed from enforced idleness through provision of work in 'healthful surroundings'.35 The enabling legislation breezed through Congress and was signed into law by FDR on March 31. Shortly after the founding of the CCC, the New Deal took its initial moves to improve unemployment relief.

While Roosevelt was assuming office, he attempted to punish big finance for its role in creating the 1929 crash. Even Herbert Hoover accused speculators of scheming to short sell other people's stock in order to profit from their own holdings. With his encouragement, the Republican-led Senate Banking and Currency Committee conducted investigations that yielded no results until Ferdinand Pecora became its lead counsel in January 1933. Pecora, the 51-year-old son of a cobbler from Sicily, had worked his way through law school to become an associate New York district attorney before going into private practice. His team of lawyers revealed that around half of the $450 billion securities issued in the free-and-easy 1920s were worthless after subpoenaing a pile of records from investment banks. Pecora scored his first major victory during cross-examination of Charles Mitchell, president of the National City Bank (forerunner of Citigroup), dubbed 'Sunshine Charley' on Wall Street for his unashamed optimism about the securities he was selling, including the worthless ones. Mitchell had pioneered the convergence of commercial banking, investment banking, and brokerage, but in eight days of evidence, he was forced to admit to his bank's security house selling bad stocks on naïve small investors and his personal tax fraud. Pecora's investigation broadened to require J.P. Morgan and other investment bankers to testify about their dubious tactics. He also discovered tax evasion by producing paper losses on stock transactions, the issuing of stock to rescue bad loans made by the parent commercial bank, and the protection of preferred clients by selling them stock at below market value.

Regulation of Wall Street became a New Deal goal as a result of the Pecora investigations. Huston Thompson, a Wilsonian Democrat and former chair of the Federal Trade Commission, drafted the Truth in Securities Act, which Roosevelt sent to Congress on March 29. The accompanying presidential message praised it for replacing the principle of caveat emptor in securities transactions by placing "the burden of telling the entire truth on the seller."45 Expert criticism of its shortcomings during House Interstate Commerce Committee hearings convinced Chairman Sam Rayburn (D-Texas) that an altogether new measure was required. When FDR adviser Raymond Moley asked Harvard law professor Felix Frankfurter for assistance, he enlisted three of his former pupils to create feasible legislation. To perform their work, New York corporate lawyer Benjamin Cohen, Reconstruction Finance Corporation staffer Tommy Corcoran, and Harvard Law School professor James Landis holed up in Washington's Carlton Hotel, one block from the White House.

On the same day he signed Glass-Steagall, a New Deal success story, FDR signed legislation establishing its least effective agency, the National Recovery Administration (NRA), founded by the Hundred Days' most hastily constructed, ill-thought-out, and unwieldy legislation. Its origins can be traced back to Roosevelt's desperate desire to prevent Congress from passing the 'thirty-hour bill,' backed by Senator Hugo Black (D-Alabama). Previously, the New Deal had not included laws to accelerate industrial employment expansion due to inconsistencies between the numerous panaceas on offer. While FDR waited for his thoughts to coalesce, Senate Democrats moved in to promote a spread-the-work law that barred goods created in firms where employees worked more than a thirty-hour week from interstate commerce.

On May 17, the president sent to Congress what became the National Industrial Recovery Act (NIRA), along with a message urging Congress to approve the necessary machinery for 'a great cooperative movement throughout all industry in order to obtain wide reemployment, to shorten the working week, to pay a decent wage for the shorter week, and to prevent unfair competition and disastrous overproduction'.53 Despite the rapidity with which the House passed the bill, Western progressives placed anti-trust clauses in the Senate version to prevent the industrial codes from becoming charters for commercial monopolies. The conference committee rejected this amendment due to corporate arguments that price fixing was necessary for recovery. On June 13, the reconciled bill was approved by the Senate by a vote of 46 to 39.

Title I of NIRA, as it was eventually approved, established the National Recovery Administration with a two-year mandate to oversee a huge process of federally sanctioned cartelization. It gave the president the final authority to adopt codes drawn up by trade groups for an entire sector as long as they were not monopolistic, to revise them as needed, and to impose a code in an industry that could not agree on one.

Title II of NIRA established the Public Works Administration (PWA) with a $3.3 billion appropriation to fund federally supported construction projects. Pump-priming advocates inside the Roosevelt administration, Frances Perkins and Rexford Tugwell, had sought a $5 billion allocation, but FDR was wary of such large expenditures, a stance reinforced by the penny-pinching Lewis Douglas. If Roosevelt had been left to his own ways, he could have persisted with the $900 million in projects selected by Herbert Hoover as deserving of federal backing.

The Hundred Days of 1933 ended with the adjournment of Congress on June 16, 1933. The legislation signed by FDR had decisively resolved the bank crisis, devised new bureaucratic structures to reorganize key sectors of the nation's economy, developed government mortgage financing to rescue hard-pressed farm owners and homeowners, launched the greatest public-works program and the most daring regional-planning experiment in American history, and built significantly on the narrow foundations of unemployment relief promulgated by Herbert Hoover. All of this added up to a record of rapid policy innovation unrivaled by any predecessor or successor - indeed, all those who took office after FDR would be assessed against his unattainable standard in their first hundred days.

Roosevelt's close relationship with the American people lasted the whole of his presidency. Another key shift in his administration was the assumption of responsibility for economic management, which was implied in the currency and gold powers granted originally by the Emergency Banking Act and later by the Thomas Amendment. Most critically, the legislative blitzkrieg of 1933 increased his office's power and authority by putting it at the center of the activist national state.

While the Hundred Days were critical to the change of the presidency, it also had unintended repercussions. FDR faced administrative coordination issues as a result of the multitude of federal agencies established to run the new programs. Their resolution eventually necessitated the formation of new executive processes within the White House in 1939, which increased the president's ability to secure bureaucracy cooperation with his aims. The early New Deal's tremendous expansion of federal authority also generated constitutional problems, putting FDR in conflict with the judicial department of government in the mid-1930s. The Supreme Court's eventual recognition of Washington's socioeconomic activism resulted in a constitutional revolution with enormous implications for presidential leadership of public affairs.

When the 1933 legislative session concluded, the New Deal was far from complete. With the exception of the election-year 1936, the next five years saw significant increases in legislative production. These projects aimed to either improve existing programs or create new ones to address disregarded or unresolved issues. As the emergency conditions of 1933 subsided, FDR would face far more difficulty in adopting administration measures without their being weakened through amendment by congressional conservatives, particularly in the case of socioeconomic policies directed at disadvantaged communities. Nonetheless, Congress would continue to rely on the president to shape its legislative agenda. This was the most important legacy of the Hundred Days.

2

New Dealer

FDR and socio-economic reform

Roosevelt characterized freedom as socioeconomic security backed by the national government in his public speeches from 1934 through 1955. This idea was best expressed in his special message to Congress in June 1934. 'Among our priorities,' he declared, 'I place the security of the Nation's men, women, and children first.' He defined 'three big objectives - the security of the house, the security of livelihood, and the security of social insurance' as 'a minimum of the promise that we can provide to the American people'. These were defined as "a right that belongs to every individual and every family willing to work." In his popular history of democratic philosophy, published in 1941, Columbia University philosopher Irwin Edman praised the New Deal's development of these aims, writing that economic security had "at last been recognized as a political condition of personal freedom."

The inability of the early New Deal to accomplish economic recovery made it necessary to redefine freedom. The National Recovery Administration (NRA) was unable to fulfill its purpose of revitalizing and reforming the industrial sector by developing industry-wide standards of fair competition to govern output levels, pricing, working hours, and wages. The job of developing charters capable of harmonizing the interests of large and small businesses, regional diversity, and capital-labor divisions was beyond it. Furthermore, the NRA took little effort to reform discriminatory hiring policies that harmed African Americans and women. To make problems worse, it was led by inept people. General Hugh Johnson's tremendous energy, thunderous oratory, and flair for cajolery suggested that he might quickly develop a new government-business alliance. Personal concerns lurked beneath his rough demeanor, manifesting themselves in bluster, bullying, and binge drinking.

Despite being an inconsistent backer of labor during the industrial struggle of 1933-4, FDR went down in history as a champion of labor. Though he was eager to help employees through NRA efforts, he was not enthused in empowering their unions, as evidenced by his stance on the contentious issue of exclusive representation. The National Labor Board, the NRA's generally ineffective mediation agency, decided on March 1, 1934, that the union that received the most votes in a government-supervised representation election had earned the exclusive right to represent all workers. This notion was effectively rejected by Roosevelt's personal intervention in another recognition conflict between the United Auto Workers and the automotive industries. On March 25, he announced a deal that provided for proportional participation rather than exclusive representation, effectively legitimizing company unions. Labor's congressional allies, led by Senator Robert Wagner (D-New York), planned to pass new legislation strengthening union rights. To put a stop to them, Roosevelt issued an executive order on June 29 that established the National Labor Relations Board (NLRB) in place of the National Labor Board. Given more authority than its predecessor, it settled the representation issue in the Houde case, ruling that any organization designated as bargaining agent by the majority of employees "had the right... to be treated by the employer as the exclusive bargaining agency of all the employees in the unit."

AAA became a house split against itself due to bureaucratic infighting. On one side stood Peek and his team of administrators, many of whom had been moved from the US Department of Agriculture (USDA). They were, at their core, agricultural industrialists committed to the interests of landlords and food processors and motivated by a single overarching concern. 'The task is straightforward,' Peek said. 'It's only to raise farm prices.' Against them was a group of young New Dealers, many of whom were Ivy League-educated lawyers with little farming experience. Their goal was to create a respectable standard of living for farm laborers, tenants, and sharecroppers of all races, not merely to recover commodity prices. The reformers were located in the AAA legal section, which was led by General Counsel Jerome Frank, a close friend of Rexford Tugwell. According to Peek, they hoped to transform AAA "from a device to aid farmers into a device to introduce the collectivist system of agriculture into this country."

Despite the dismissal of Peek, AAA remained divided over whether its aim was economic or social. Voluntary participation in its production-control program was enticed by financial bonuses to farm owners who lowered output. In order to raise commodity prices by bringing supply in line with demand, the USDA's Bureau of Agricultural Economics calculates the area to be removed from cultivation for each major crop and sets livestock objectives each year. It also determined how much the federal government would compensate for agricultural production losses. The AAA was then confronted with the enormous task of issuing millions of individual contracts to participating farmers outlining their acreage and commodity reduction requirements, as well as their cash recompense for satisfying these duties. It could only do so by enlisting the assistance of pre-existing institutions, both governmental and non-governmental, that were already heavily involved in the farm economy.

These lovely words belied the fact that the AAA made no provision for the 4.5 million agricultural laborers, sharecroppers, and renters who make up roughly one-third of the agrarian workforce. Landowners were supposed to share their federal advantages with them, but few did. Many sharecroppers and renters were evicted in the cotton South by owners striving to meet AAA acreage-reduction obligations. In Arkansas, they fought back by joining the inter-racial Southern Tenant Farmers Union (STFU), only to be driven into submission by the whips and guns of the local cotton lords' 'riding bosses' and police lackeys. Norman Thomas, a regular Socialist Party presidential candidate, traveled to the White House to seek Roosevelt's intervention after being beaten while advocating for the union in the ill-named hamlet of Birdsong. FDR, reliant on Southern

Democrats in Congress, unwilling to jeopardize the entire New Deal for the sake of the STFU. 'Now come, Norman, I'm a darn sight better politician than you are,' he said. I know the South, and a new generation of leaders is emerging, but we must be patient.'

Shedding social-mission goals may have rescued AAA from legislative conservatives' wrath, but the agency was caught up in the Supreme Court's wider attack on the New Deal.

Following the Supreme Court's reversal on the constitutionality of the New Deal, Roosevelt's agriculture policy began a third phase with the passage of the Agricultural Adjustment Act of 1938. This began the process of constructing an ever-normal granary (government acquisition of surplus commodities to protect against future crop failures), made soil conservation a permanent program, authorized crop loans, and provided wheat producers with drought insurance.

Despite setbacks, the New Deal succeeded in stabilizing the agrarian economy by the conclusion of FDR's second term, preventing it from suffering again.

Hopkins created the CWA bureaucracy from scratch after Roosevelt established it through executive order on November 9, 1933. CWA prioritized the self-worth and dignity of the unemployed, hiring half of its workers from relief lists and half from the poor unemployed without a means test. Instead of gifts, it paid a wage at the prevailing minimum rate (40 cents an hour in the South, 60 cents an hour in the North).

FDR liked Hopkins' accomplishments but was concerned about the financial and social ramifications. On 23 January 1934, he told the National Emergency Council that if the CWA lasted throughout the summer, it would "become a habit with the country…

The legislation established the Securities and Exchange Commission (SEC), gave it discretionary authority to regulate approximately twenty stock exchanges, required listed companies to file detailed financial reports with the SEC, limited the ability of floor traders and insiders to manipulate the market, and empowered the Federal Reserve to regulate margin requirements for stock trading on credit. '[T]he fundamental problem with this entire Stock Exchange crowd is their complete lack of rudimentary education,' FDR wrote to Adolf Berle, one of the bill's intellectual influences. I don't mean a lack of college certificates or anything like that, but rather an incapacity to grasp the country, the people, or their responsibilities to their fellow man.'

While the New Deal sought recovery and regulatory change in the second half of the Depression, Roosevelt's annual message to Congress in January 1935 signaled a shift in priorities. Declaring that social justice... has become a definite goal,' he outlined specific steps to achieve this. 'We seek [change] through tested liberal traditions, through processes that retain all of the basic essentials of that republican system of representative government first entrusted to a troubled globe by the United States,' Roosevelt said.

WPA put able-bodied assistance recipients to work on long-term, self-sustaining, labor-intensive projects. The 1.5 million FERA participants who were too sick, aged, or disabled to work were returned to the care of local institutions, the majority of which lacked the capacity to offer proper assistance. Meanwhile, at least five million unemployed people who were not on aid rolls were left out of the reach of federal assistance. Over the course of its eight-year existence, the WPA employed 8.5 million people at a cost of around $11 billion, with a peak enrollment of 3.3 million in late 1938.4Because half of the labor-force participants aged sixteen to twenty-four were unemployed, FDR established the National Youth Administration as a WPA auxiliary. To encourage needy students to stay in school or college, it provided them stipends to do on-campus work, which reached 400,000 students by 1937.

The formation of the WPA as an independent agency under Harry Hopkins sparked a legal battle with Harold Ickes, who wanted it for his PWA empire. To quell their rivalry, Roosevelt decided that projects costing less than $25,000 should go to the WPA and those costing more should go to the PWA, but the astute Hopkins remained one step ahead of his opponent.

To soothe presidential concerns, the CES created a hybrid financing structure based on a 1% payroll tax divided 50/50 between workers and businesses, eventually increasing to a total 5% in 1956. This would pay for more generous payments to early retirees than their contributions deserved, with the remainder coming from a one-time federal appropriation in the mid-1960s, after which the program would become self-sufficient. The unexpected intervention of Henry Morgenthau spurred additional modifications. Despite signing off on the final CES report, he launched a personal campaign opposing any federal subsidization of contributory insurance as a tax fraud. The Treasury Secretary persuaded FDR that the payroll tax should begin at 2%, divided equally by employers and employees, in order to accumulate a reserve of roughly $50 billion by 1980, relieving the federal government of its future commitment.

The law was redrafted and passed the House of Representatives by 372 votes to 33 in April, and the Senate by 77 votes to 6 in June. The Social Security Act of 1935, as finally approved in reconciled form, provided for unemployment insurance, old-age pensions, and categorical assistance (funded through a combination of general taxes and matching state grants) for specific groups, including fatherless families with dependent children, the blind, the physically handicapped, and the indigent elderly. When Roosevelt signed the bill on August 14, he admitted that it "represents a cornerstone in a structure that is being built but is by no means complete."60 The SSA, without a doubt the most important piece of social legislation in US history, laid the groundwork for a peculiarly American welfare state that established a two-tier system based on social security, which rewarded recipients for working, and public assistance, which provided limited aid to those who were unable to work.

The SSA was the most significant of five major legislation and a slew of lesser but nonetheless crucial ones passed during what became known as the second Hundred Days' in Washington, lasting from early June to late August 1935. At the end of May, few people would have predicted this conclusion. At the time, the 'Big Bill' was FDR's only notable legislative achievement. Despite the midterm reform mandate, Roosevelt found himself on the defensive in the face of an anti-lynch law filibuster and the New Deal's unclear constitutional status. Harold Ickes admitted in his notebook that the president needed to reaffirm the posture of aggressive leadership he had demonstrated in 1933.

Another of Roosevelt's Must' legislation aimed primarily at the wealthy. After previously opposing any additional taxes to create revenue, he startled Congress with a letter advocating for a wealth tax. This was his sole initiative in reaction to the Long-Coughlin grassroots agitation on his 1935 agenda.

Roosevelt acquiesced to congressional modifications without objection after laying down his marker. The final legislation established additional rates for annual incomes above $1 million, ending in a top band of 79% for individuals earning more than $5 million, a levy that only affected one man in the country - oil billionaire John D. Rockefeller. It established a minor estate tax rather than the harsh inheritance tax proposed by FDR, enhanced gift taxes, and imposed a minimal business tax. The proposal was a flop in terms of wealth redistribution, taking nothing of note from the richest 1% while completely ignoring others with lesser but nonetheless large fortunes. It fit well with FDR's successful re-election campaign tactic of slamming economic elites in political terms, but it was harmful in another way.

The intense pace of the second Hundred Days tired Roosevelt physically and emotionally. Weariness may have influenced his answer to Roy Howard, head of the Scripps-Howard newspaper network, who urged a "pause from further experimentation" to restore corporate confidence. FDR responded that the administration's "basic program" had "now reached substantial completion, and the "breathing spell" of which you speak is here - very decisively so." He most likely planned for the hiatus to extend until re-election offered a mandate for additional reforms to assist low-income Americans.

The latter New Deal similarly fell short of its goal of assisting urban renters. FDR told the National Emergency Council in late 1934 that he wanted to help the forty million people who lacked adequate housing, but he resisted advocating Robert Wagner's public-housing legislation for over three years.

The Fair Labor Standards Act (FLSA) of 1938 was Roosevelt's most major second-term measure to improve the economic security of low-income Americans. Another Cohen-Corcoran collaboration, the initial bill submitted in Congress in May 1937 promised workers involved in interstate commerce a 'living wage' for a workweek with fixed maximum hours, enforceable by the Labor Standards Board, a new organization with broad powers. A much-amended and weaker bill, with supervision authority transferred to the Department of Labor rather than a powerful new organization, was finally enacted fourteen months later. To keep their region's low-wage structure as an incentive for corporate relocation from elsewhere in the country, Southern Democrats pushed on minimum-wage guarantees of only 25 cents an hour, rather than the initially planned 40 cents. Despite its repeal, the FLSA instantly increased salaries for around 300,000 employees, reduced working hours for 1 million workers, and barred child labor. However, its benefits did not extend to workers who were not involved in interstate commerce, most notably farm labor and domestic servants, vocations dominated by African Americans and women, respectively.

Roosevelt's increasing difficulties in enacting New Deal measures that aided Americans in the lower half of the income distribution from the mid-1930s onward provided a more accurate gauge of his transformation of the president's role as chief legislator than the heady successes of the Hundred Days of 1933. Congress reasserted its obligations, as historian Ira Katznelson put it, "as a forum where detailed answers could be created to the main substantive challenges of a historically dense and difficult era."

When Congress left the recovery effort nearly totally in the hands of the president during the 1933 crisis, it still asserted its right to shape the legislative outputs that resulted from Roosevelt's suggestions.

Roosevelt's use of the presidential pulpit to shape popular support boosted his capacity to persuade Congress to do his bidding during his first term. Roosevelt's policy blunders hampered his success as a public communicator during his second administration. The planned reform of the Supreme Court in 1937, as well as the advent of the 1937-8 harsh recession, harmed his popularity, promoting the creation of bipartisan conservative opposition in Congress. By late 1938, the New Deal's legislative reform effort had completely run its course. As the economy recovered from the Great Depression, FDR knew that the most immediate method to improve the lives of millions of Americans was to get them into well-paying jobs.

3

Second emancipator

FDR and African Americans

Many African Americans saw FDR as a second emancipator who had done more for their race than any president since Abraham Lincoln. They were accustomed to government indifference of their needs, thus the New Deal provided tremendous socioeconomic help.

The Great Depression further disenfranchised African Americans, who were already economically marginalized. In 1930, half of them lived in the rural South, where four-fifths worked as tenant farmers, sharecroppers, and wage laborers. With cotton prices falling, many people left the countryside to seek work in Dixie's towns, where they found whites working in positions that were traditionally considered Black, such as cleaners, janitors, and road sweepers. Those who migrated north fared no better; in early 1933, black male unemployment in New York, Philadelphia, Chicago, and Detroit averaged more than 40%, while female unemployment was considerably worse at 55%.

FDR owed African Americans nothing for his election, thus he had no motivation to prioritize their needs and every reason to avoid irritating Southern Democrats whose support he needed in Congress. He agreed with long-time adviser Louis Howe on the importance of favoring 'our Southern brethren' over 'our worried Negro brethren'. FDR, determined to focus on economic rather than racial issues, was certain on one point: 'First things come first, and I can't alienate certain votes I need for measures that are more critical at the moment by pressing any policies that would entail a battle.' Except for Secretary of the Interior Harold Ickes, none of the Cabinet or agency chiefs disagreed. When certain New Dealers became more outspoken about race, Roosevelt had no qualms about correcting them on the facts as he perceived them.

The Civilian Conservation Corps (CCC), which was founded to place unemployed and unmarried young men to work on natural-resource conservation projects, fell short of the anti-discriminatory principles of the legislation that authorized it. Young Blacks saw it as an excellent opportunity to learn new skills and earn money.

The early New Deal, as epitomized by the CCC, tended to entrench rather than alleviate racial separation. The Tennessee Valley Authority, ostensibly an experiment in decentralized 'grass-roots democracy,' separated workers in its numerous projects and towns. The Federal Housing Administration refused to insure dwellings in areas of Black settlement in America's cities and encouraged the almost entirely white recipients of its assistance to preserve neighborhood property values by enacting restrictive covenants prohibiting the sale of their home to Blacks. The Public Works Administration (PWA) was the single agency that practiced racial equity. It implemented racial quotas for private contractors on its projects under the direction of Harold Ickes, a former president of the NAACP's Chicago chapter, based on the percentage of African Americans in the local workforce as documented in the 1930 occupational census. Centralized control of contract adherence resulted in greater hiring of Black laborers, who came to associate PWA with the phrase "Pop's Working Again."

FDR's racial record was heavily criticized by the African-American elite two years into his presidency. In the larger Black community, however, feeling was solidly in favor of FDR. Whereas African-American elites were preoccupied with the racial dimension of the "Negro problem," the Black masses were preoccupied with economic problems.

The WPA assisted many more African Americans, including men and women, than any other New Deal initiative. While the majority were hired as manual laborers, some acquired skilled employment, others were hired as architects, engineers, and medical personnel, and still others were hired as authors, musicians, actresses, and artists through the Federal Project Number One program. WPA built public facilities such as schools and recreation centers that improved the lives of many Black communities, enrolled Blacks of all ages in education and vocational training courses, helped nearly 250,000 achieve literacy, and established nursery programs for Black children, in addition to providing jobs.

In 1934, the NAACP launched a strong push to enact an anti-lynching bill developed under its auspices, with extensive support from religious and civic organizations. This penalized law enforcement officers who failed to prevent lynchings, authorized federal prosecution of lynchers if state officials were unwilling to do so within thirty days of the offence, and imposed fines of up to $10,000 on counties where the crime occurred, payable to the victim's dependents. The bill, sponsored by Senators Edward Costigan (D-Colorado) and Robert Wagner (D-New York), was reported out of the Senate Judiciary Committee with minor amendments in March 1934, but it faced filibustering on the Senate floor by Southern Democrats. Senate Majority Leader Joseph Robinson (D-Arkansas), unwilling to obstruct the chamber's work, refused to call the bill up for debate.

A legislative maneuver eventually got the bill before the entire Senate in April 1935, but at the expense of inciting a Southern filibuster that stalled consideration of crucial New Deal initiatives such as social insurance. Northern and Western Democrats agreed with their Southern colleagues to adjourn debate without a vote in response to presidential exhortations to get back to work. White resigned from the Advisory Council for the Government of the Virgin Islands in protest.

4

Constitutional revolutionary

FDR and the Supreme Court

Franklin D. Roosevelt engineered a constitutional revolution that kept the New Deal from being overturned by the courts. Roosevelt had a healthy regard for the Constitution as a living constitution that could be constantly reinterpreted as circumstances dictated. In 1930, he said that America's supreme law "has proven itself the most marvelously elastic compilation of rules of government ever written."

As a result, Roosevelt was not going to take judicial challenges to the New Deal's constitutionality lying down. As Robert Jackson put it, "his motives were always good for the things that he wanted to do," and "he found difficulty in thinking that there could be legal limitations on them." To FDR, the Constitution was a tool for furthering the general good, not an ossified guarantee of limited government.

Because he was preoccupied with the economic crisis, FDR did not make it a personal priority to establish a Justice Department capable of serving as the New Deal's constitutional bulwark. He entrusted this obligation to Senator Thomas Walsh (D-Montana), an experienced Washington insider whom he appointed as Attorney General, but the old Westerner died two days before Inauguration Day from a heart attack. Roosevelt named Homer Cummings as a temporary stand-in on the advice of Marguerite LeHand. Cummings, a former Democratic National Committee (DNC) chairman, was a Connecticut state attorney and Roosevelt supporter in 1932. His intuitive sense that FDR wanted an Attorney General who could give legal support for New Deal measures led to his permanent appointment. 'Homer is a fine fellow,' a grateful FDR once said. He's always coming up with new methods to do things.'

FDR was significantly more concerned about the impending decision on the constitutionality of the repeal of the gold clause in any contract, private or public, enacted by Congress in June 1933. The Supreme Court heard three days of arguments in the Gold Clause cases in early January 1935, but did not issue its findings until 18 February. The uncertainty in the interim weeks cast a greater shadow over the White House than anything since the March 1933 banking crisis. If the verdict was reversed, the clamor of public bondholders for windfall payments in gold, which is now more than two-thirds more expensive in dollar terms than it was in 1933, would erode federal solvency and deplete the New Deal's fiscal resources. In anticipation of a negative verdict, FDR prepared a radio address in which he stated his resolve not to be bound by it.

Far worse was to come for Roosevelt on May 27, the New Deal's Black Monday, when the Supreme Court issued three unanimous opinions that appeared to amount to a judicial declaration of war on his government. Humphrey's Executor v. US reversed the removal of William Humphrey, a Calvin Coolidge appointment to the Federal Trade Commission, in 1933. The administration's defense, urged by Stanley Reed in his first case as Solicitor General, was based on the Taft Court's decision in Myers v. United States (1926) over a postmaster's dismissal that the president had unlimited power of removal over executive-branch staff. Rejecting this precedent, the Hughes Court ruled that Humphrey could only be removed as a member of an independent regulatory board with the consent of Congress.

In addressing three concerns with enormous consequences for the entire New Deal, the Chief Justice wrote a unanimous judgment that sentenced the NRA to death. First, while unusual economic conditions may necessitate extraordinary responses, they did not "create or expand constitutional power." Second, Congress was not entitled to delegate its legislative responsibilities to the president by broad delegation of undefined authority to issue public rules with the force of law in regulating private economic activity. Finally, the 'commerce authority' could not be applied to enterprises that primarily conducted intrastate rather than interstate operations. Even the progressive members of the Supreme Court decided the time had come to draw a line against unchecked government power expansion. '[T]ell your President that this Court has told him it is not going to countenance the centralization of power which his advisors are imposing on our country,' an irritated Louis Brandeis cautioned presidential assistant Thomas Corcoran.

Roosevelt warned reporters that resolving the impasse could take five to ten years. This meant that his solution was a constitutional amendment to limit the ability of the courts to invalidate laws passed by Congress. To gauge public sentiment, FDR dictated entire paragraphs for an article published in Collier's in September under the pen name of journalist George Creel. The president would have no choice if the Supreme Court continued to render "the current generation powerless to meet social and economic problems that were not within the knowledge of the founding fathers."

While the Hughes Court was unable to recreate the unanimity of Black Monday in its 1936 session, the majority of judges demonstrated that they were not about to back down. The AAA was slain in a six-to-three decision in US v. Butler on January 6. The majority judgment, written at the request of the Chief Justice, agreed that Congress might spend "public money for public purposes," including the "general welfare," a crucial reinforcement of New Deal spending programs. In the case of AAA, however, it distinguished between 'commerce,' which Congress could regulate, and 'production,' which came before commerce and was subject to state regulation under Amendment X of the Constitution. It also ruled that the processing tax used to fund AAA production-control payments to farmers was an unlawful 'expropriation of money from one group for the benefit of another' rather than a real tax to produce income. Harlan Stone argued in a vehement dissent that judges should be concerned with the constitutionality of legislation rather than its wisdom. He cautioned that courts "are not the only agency of government that must be assumed to have capacity to govern." Far from displeasing Roosevelt, these decisions added grist to his conviction that the judicial branch would eventually be hoisted with its anti-New Deal petard.

When FDR chose to sue the Supreme Court, his masterful political touch failed him. Cloaking his aims in secrecy to avoid leaks, he cut out experienced lawyers from discussing the hazards of the court-packing scheme. Framing one of the most radical propositions presented to Congress by any president as a common-sense reform to boost judicial efficiency was clearly deceptive. His worst blunder was his arrogant expectation that the voters who had returned him to office in a landslide would blindly support him on Supreme Court change.

The three-horse metaphor for the distinct institutions of government was reiterated in a Fireside Chat on March 9, the start of his second administration. FDR, identifying himself as a horse rather than the driver, declared, 'It is the American people themselves who are in the driver's seat... who want the furrow plowed... who expect the third horse to pull alongside the other two.' 'To defend the Constitution from the Court, and the Court from itself,' it was now required. The remedy was to select additional justices who were sensitive to the needs of the country as a counterbalance to "the personal judgment of a few men who, fearful of the future, would envy us the necessary means of dealing with the present."

Hughes led the court to a five-four rejection of Tipaldo in the West Coast v. Parrish decision, which upheld a Washington state minimum-wage statute. The judgment, issued on March 29 but really decided in January, was a response to the 1936 vote rather than FDR's yet-unlaunched judicial attack, though it was never acknowledged as such. Roberts' switch from the Tipaldo majority to the Parrish majority marked a constitutional somersault that turned the sanctity of contract freedom on its head. He then joined Hughes, Brandeis, Cardozo, and Stone in rulings that upheld key New Deal legislation. On April 12, four decisions upheld the National Labor Relations Act of 1935, each by a five-four majority. The most important case, National Labor Relations Board v. Jones & Laughlin Steel Corp., held that Congress had the jurisdiction to regulate intrastate commerce that directly affected interstate activity.

In desperation, Robinson exploited Senate rules to schedule a floor debate on the new bill on July 6. His prospects hinged on assembling a coalition of New Deal stalwarts, undecided Democrats loyal to him, and the 1936 rookie class elected on FDR's coattails. He bore the primary task of advocating for the bill on the floor and negotiating votes behind closed doors in the days that followed. The difficult effort, conducted in the blazing July heat of Washington, proved too much for the 65-year-old. Robinson died of a heart attack in his flat in the Methodist building across Maryland Avenue from the Supreme Court building on the 14th of July. He died, and so did the hopes for the updated judicial bill. When the Senate reconvened following his funeral in Little Rock, it overwhelmingly voted to recommit the legislation to committee, from which it never emerged.

FDR selected Stanley Reed to fill the vacancy left by George Sutherland's retirement in January 1938. On June 12, 1941, Roosevelt found himself in the unusual position of having to make three Supreme Court selections. He started by appointing Harlan Stone to succeed retiring Charles Evans Hughes.At the start of 1941, the last of the Four Horsemen rode off into angry retirement. The 79-year-old justice, who despises Roosevelt, had sworn 'never [to] resign as long as that handicapped son-of-a-bitch is in the White House,' but the president's victory to a third term dashed that desire.69 In his place, FDR selected James Byrnes as a reward for his dedication to pushing administration programs in the Senate, most recently in his floor handling of the Lend-Lease legislation.

Roosevelt completed his trio of choices by nominating Robert Jackson as Associate Justice to fill Stone's seat. Jackson is the first person to have served as Solicitor General, Attorney General, and Supreme Court justice before the age of fifty, having qualified for the bar by apprenticeship in an attorney's office rather than law school.

By the time the United States entered the war, the Supreme Court had become an ally rather than an adversary of New Deal socioeconomic control. Internal schisms made its record on rights-based jurisprudence less apparent, but the momentum remained in favor of stronger civil liberties protection.

5

Party leader

FDR and the Democrats

Roosevelt inherited a Democratic Party that lacked a defined political identity, had a restricted base, and was internally split. FDR's opposite opinion that a new political majority could only be developed within the current party system was motivated by the failure of Progressive third-party campaigns in 1912 and 1924. According to his perspective, the Great Depression improved the political atmosphere for the Democratic transformation project that he first envisioned in the 1920s.

Despite winning one of the largest electoral victories in American history, many analysts regarded it as a qualified victory due to Roosevelt's nonpartisan attitude on the campaign trail. The political realignment foretold in the elections of 1928 and 1932 came to fulfillment during FDR's first term, with the formation of a new voting coalition whose constituent members and allied interest groups were direct benefactors of New Deal liberalism. This accomplishment came at the expense of fostering dissatisfaction among traditional Democratic constituents and organizations, which erupted into intra-party strife during Roosevelt's second term.

Another important component of the Roosveltian Democratic Party was organized labor. Before the 1930s, the American Federation of Labor (AFL)'s craft-based unions displayed only occasional partisanship. The labor reforms reflected in the National Industrial Recovery Act of 1933, and more broadly in the National Labor Relations Act of 1935, transformed unions into an essential component of the New Deal alliance. Teamsters president Daniel Tobin offered leadership stability to the organization as chair of the

DNC Labour Division, but the divide that emerged between craft and industrial unions hampered coordination of their political operations. Fearing that broad unionization might undermine its grip on the labor movement, the AFL suspended the ten unions that had created the Committee (later Congress) of Industrial Organizations (CIO) to spearhead the organization of unskilled and semi-skilled workers in September 1936. Because Tobin was an AFL vice-chairman, the CIO refused to work through the DNC Labour Division. Two of its leaders, John L. Lewis of the United Mine Workers and Sidney Hillman of the Amalgamated Clothing Workers, founded the Nonpartisan League to promote New Deal Democrats.

In his encounters with urban party groups, Roosevelt's animosity to New York City's regular Democrats was the exception rather than the rule. He was friendly with metropolitan executives such as Edward Kelly in Chicago, Frank Hague in Jersey City, Ed Crump in Memphis, and Tom Prendergast in Kansas City (until his conviction for income tax evasion landed him in a federal prison). New Deal programs aided in the formation of new Democratic machines in previously Republican cities such as Philadelphia and Pittsburgh. The Works Progress Administration gave supervisory employment for the majority of its Democratic ward chairmen and precinct captains in addition to spending $70 million for work relief in Pittsburgh's Allegheny County in its first two years of existence.

Roosevelt staffed the New Deal agencies with a pool of well-educated, young, idealistic lawyers and academics established by his informal aides, Thomas Corcoran and Benjamin Cohen, in order to build an executive-led administrative state. This technique of recruitment resulted in what one enthusiastic analyst described as a "psychological "blood transfusion" that "invigorated political administration beyond belief."

Roosevelt ran a broad-based effort in 1932 to gain business backing for an activist government, but four years later he started a political war on corporate America. The opposing party in this dispute was already waging a full-fledged assault on the New Deal. After hailing FDR as a savior in 1933, the majority of the country's leading business people saw him as a traitor to his class within two years. The American Liberty League (ALL), co-founded in 1934 by former DNC head John Raskob, was in the vanguard of the business campaign, backed by a bipartisan alliance of conservatives with significant corporate ties and funded by the Du Pont family.

Some polls anticipated a close contest as the election neared, but their methodology was untrustworthy. James Farley famously predicted that FDR would win every state except Maine and Vermont. This result gave him the greatest Electoral College majority in history, 523 to 8. His popular vote share of 60.8 percent and eleven million vote margin over Landon set new highs. Presidential coat-tails aided Democrats in gaining historic majorities in the House (333 seats to 89) and the Senate (76 seats to 16). Roosevelt carried the country as a whole, making his victory a national one. Approximately 20% of his support came from individuals who typically identified as Republicans. He captured over five million of the six million increase in turnout over 1932, doing particularly well among first-time voters. His margins were better than 2 to 1 in Baltimore, Chicago, Cleveland, Detroit, and Los Angeles, 3 to 1 in San Francisco and New York, 4 to 1 in Milwaukee, and even larger in Southern metropolises like Atlanta, Birmingham, and Houston. His plurality in becoming the first Democrat to carry Pennsylvania since 1856 was built on enormous majorities in Philadelphia (where he received 60.5 percent of the vote) and Pittsburgh.

The greatest challenge to the New Deal in FDR's first term came from the Supreme Court; in his second, it came from conservative Democrats in Congress, aided in second-fiddle by conservative Republicans. Conservative Democrats came from all over the country, mostly from rural districts and states, and hated Roosevelt's expanding ties to urban liberalism.

In the months that followed, Roosevelt endorsed liberal-leaning Democrats facing conservative primary opponents. On his way west to take a Pacific cruise vacation in July, he stopped in several places to express support for Senator Alben Barkley (D-Kentucky), Senator Hattie Caraway (D-Arkansas), Senator Elmer Thomas (D-Oklahoma), and Representative Lyndon B. Johnson (D-Texas), all of whom won their primary elections. Roosevelt certainly wished he had gone out of his way to support Senator James Pope (D-Idaho), a New Deal devotee who was nearly beaten by a conservative primary challenger. Nonetheless, as Representative Maury Maverick (D-Texas) and Senator William Gibbs McAdoo (D-California) discovered, his approval did not guarantee success, and the latter was defeated by a leftist rival.

The only achievement of the purging campaign was the removal of Representative John O'Connor (D-New York), who had stalled New Deal legislation as chair of the Rules Committee. In an urban area dominated by low-income voters, the president's endorsement of his opponent, James Fay, had more weight. Whereas the Senate purges were half-measures, FDR advisers worked methodically to undermine O'Connor. The New Republic gushed, "This single victory is enough to justify the entire [purge] effort." Following the failed purges, the Republican midterm recovery made the future of liberalism, which had seemed so solid two years before, appear 'full of peril and uncertainty' to The New Republic. Due to the unpopularity of the new farm bill, farmers outside the South were the first to abandon the Roosevelt voting coalition.

Even though FDR's political prospects had plummeted in the aftermath of the midterm elections, he had not given up on his party-transformation agenda. Accepting an honorary degree at the University of North Carolina, he declared that liberalism would "come to life again with more strength than... before." Because there was no electable liberal to continue the New Deal battle, FDR had no choice but to run himself in 1940. FDR most likely decided to run after the Nazi blitzkrieg revolutionized the war in Europe, but developments outside arguably reaffirmed rather than fueled his resolve. Since the midterm elections, the imperative to sustain Democratic liberalism had been propelling him inexorably towards a third-term run.

FDR sought Henry Wallace, a New Deal veteran, as his running mate to ensure an all-liberal ticket. When working on Wallace's behalf in various state delegations, FDR encouraged his managers to express his threat. Despite the fact that the war in Europe had taken a catastrophic turn with the fall of France just weeks before, this story demonstrated the importance of domestic political concerns in FDR's choice to run in 1940. He also told Senator George Norris that he accepted the nomination to prevent conservative Democrats from regaining control of the party.

Willkie, a former Democrat who supported Roosevelt in 1932, campaigned on a program that virtually legitimized New Deal reforms in acknowledgement of popular support. Instead of criticizing the New Deal's socio economic reforms, Willkie accused it of stifling private enterprise's ability to achieve full recovery from the Great Depression, but the continuous development of defense-related jobs throughout 1940 undermined this narrative. In desperation, he accused Roosevelt of intending to enter the war against Germany if re-elected, which increased his poll numbers.

Despite surveys indicating a close race, Roosevelt emerged as the clear winner. He won the Electoral College by 449 votes to 82, and the popular vote by 54.7 percent to 44.8 percent (Willkie added Indiana, Michigan, Iowa, both Dakotas, Nebraska, Kansas, and Colorado to Landon's Maine and Vermont). Despite Roosevelt's 'Safe on Third' status, this was his tightest victory to date.

6

Communicator-in-chief

FDR's public presidency

One of Roosevelt's deepest convictions was his belief in the wisdom of an informed public. His public presidency fulfilled two vital civic education purposes: informing the general public about the overall objectives and policies of their government, and acting as a channel for the interchange of ideas amongst them. In a speech to a Jackson Day luncheon in 1936, FDR praised "the rebirth of a great citizenry's interest and understanding in the problems of the nation." Two years later, he declared his belief that "in the long run, the instincts of the common man... work out the best for the common good." In Roosevelt's opinion, the biggest threat to this ideal form of governance was the ability of unfriendly publishers to use their publications to provide biased coverage of his administration. The owners of what FDR referred to as the "Tory press" hampered the free flow of information from the president to the people, impeding his Jeffersonian responsibilities as a civic educator. Roosevelt was fond of claiming that 85% of the newspapers - "the famous eighty-five percent," as he derisively referred to them - were against him, a charge repeated by others in his entourage, although this distorted the complexities of press opinion. Newspaper proprietors overwhelmingly praised FDR's early leadership in addressing the economic crisis.

On the other hand, despite momentary lapses, Roy Howard, leader of the Scripps-Howard chain, which held over forty daily titles and the UP-wire service, was frequently in the president's defense. The influential and independently owned New York Times editorial board backed FDR significantly more frequently than it opposed him. Roosevelt also had the support of independent publishers such as Marshall Field (owner of the Chicago Sun, founded in 1941),

Ralph Ingersoll (publisher of the New York daily PM, founded in 1940 with Field's backing), David Stern (publisher of The Philadelphia Record and, from 1933 to 1939, the New York Post), and Dorothy Schiff (who purchased the latter in 1939).

Nonetheless, FDR received significantly more popular support than press backing, particularly during election seasons. In 1932, he received 57% of the popular vote but only 41% of dailies and 45% of weeklies' editorial support; four years later, the figures were 61% compared to 37% and 40%, respectively; and the gap widened to its widest level since Jefferson's day in 1940, when Roosevelt's 55% vote share contrasted with his 25% editorial support among daily newspapers and 33% among weekly ones. Getting the facts to the public while avoiding the real or imagined enmity of newspaper publishers was critical in Roosevelt's calculation for mobilizing their support. Stephen Early's nomination as presidential Press Secretary was vital to this mission. This was the first formally titled designation of the office, which had been held by all-purpose presidential assistants since William McKinley's time.

FDR's most crucial way of incorporating the press into his public-communications strategy were regular news conferences. By bringing together the president and Washington correspondents in what one termed a "holy newslock," he made all of his predecessors appear "like Trappists who didn't even talk to themselves." The majority of press conferences were held in the Oval Office, where FDR sat behind the big presidential desk.

On the morning of March 8, 1933, Roosevelt held his first news conference, laying out four ground rules for participating correspondents: all stories based on news announcements were to be without quotation, direct quotations required the press secretary's written permission, background information given to help reporters was not to be attributed to the White House, and anything designated off-the-record was to be confidential, released only to those journalists praising Roosevelt. To maximize FDR's prospects of front-page publicity in both afternoon and morning newspapers, the Oval Office press briefings alternated between 10.30 a.m. and 4 p.m. on Wednesdays (later Tuesdays) and Fridays.

Another element that contributed to Roosevelt's favorable treatment in news articles, even in editorially unfriendly media, was his popularity with Washington journalists. Roosevelt was more accessible and cordial with journalists than any of his predecessors. FDR's encounters with Washington correspondents were part of a larger news management strategy. He prepared meticulously for the press conferences that served as the focal point of his relationship with journalists, seeing their friendliness as a counterweight to their bosses' hostility.

Roosevelt was as brilliant at non-communication as he was at communication, and he employed evasive strategies to avoid discussing topics he did not want to discuss. He refused to answer 'iffy' questions that required speculation; he rarely allowed follow-up questions to those he had not fully answered - 'no cross-examination,' he would say; sometimes he simply refused to answer a question by claiming to have no knowledge of the subject; and on occasion he was untruthful. Though some journalists were irritated by the evasions, few stopped attending Roosevelt's press conferences since he never sent the press away empty-handed.

What made Roosevelt's effectiveness as a public speaker even more surprising was that, with the exception of the Fireside Chats, he delivered most of his major speeches from a standing position. He stayed upright thanks to leg braces and leaning on a podium. Despite regular broadcasts of his other speeches, FDR's radio presidency was defined by the Fireside Chats, which were original, intimate, and casual in their use of the medium. They were hired to explain policy, report on changes, and reassure people about progress. Above all, Roosevelt used them to gain the trust of the American people so that they could understand his intentions. Despite being a quiet guy who kept his inner self buried, FDR was astonishingly successful at forging a sense of closeness with the listener during the Fireside Chats.

The first Fireside Chat, conducted from the Oval Office on March 12, 1933, had the greatest immediate influence in rebuilding public trust in institutions that had gotten federal authority to reopen. The address began, 'My friends, I want to chat for a few minutes with the people of the United States about banking.' FDR discussed how banks worked in terms of investing deposits for the advantage of listeners who largely utilized them for modest savings and checking accounts. He then described the causes of the current financial crisis, the need for federal intervention, and his plans. He reiterated that the government would reopen every bank found to be sound, even if ongoing checks on their solvency prevented some from resuming operations the next day, but he also admitted that some would fall short of the required criteria. Not every Fireside Chat had the same impact on FDR's listeners. The popular reaction to President Franklin D. Roosevelt's speech in support of restructuring the Supreme Court on March 9, 1937, was negative.

Roosevelt recreated five-minute highlights of the Fireside Chats for newsreel cameras to amplify their impact. The newsreels were more than just supplements to FDR's public presidency's Fireside Chats. They transformed him into a vivid, fully animated, moving, and talking presence for moviegoers. Even his impairment became a cinematic benefit because he was filmed speaking directly to the viewer, generally from behind a desk, rather than orating from a lectern to an auditorium.

Despite these image-control measures, FDR was eager to hear the honest thoughts of regular Americans about him. During his twelve-year presidency, Roosevelt's principal conduit into the public imagination was the millions of letters he received from people from all walks of life. His presidential library has fifteen million books, and the National Archives has millions more. While the letters and mail summaries he received offered FDR an idea of what Americans believed, he became increasingly interested in quantitative facts to back this up. His use of press conferences, radio, newsreels, travel, and popular correspondence analysis expanded on the public-presidency initiatives of his predecessors in the twentieth century, but his use of opinion polling broke new ground.

7

Chief diplomat

FDR as foreign policy leader

Franklin D. Roosevelt desired that the United States take the lead in constructing a liberal, rules-based international system that would foster long-term peace and prosperity. He saw America's interests as global in scope, requiring a foreign policy of engagement with allies, support for collective security, and promotion of democratic values overseas. The most difficult difficulty he had as chief diplomat in promoting this agenda was managing public opinion at home. The American people desired to avoid any new wars in Europe or Asia, and this feeling was shared by Congress. As a result, throughout the mid-1930s neutrality discussions, Roosevelt was second fiddle to the legislature. Following the Munich crisis in 1938, he became increasingly vocal in his support for Anglo-French resistance to Nazi expansion. Nonetheless, as war broke out in Europe, he was wary of getting too far ahead of home opinion. The triumph of Adolf Hitler's blitzkrieg of 1940, which resulted in the collapse of France, persuaded most Americans that they needed to assist Britain in order to avoid their own country going to war. Building on this, Roosevelt negotiated the implementation of the Lend-Lease program in March 1941, which provided weapons to the financially strained United Kingdom. Following that, he engaged in incremental confrontation with Hitler until the Japanese assault on Pearl Harbor forced the US into a war of necessity rather than choice. His handling of the worldwide crisis provided the groundwork for popular support for his wartime strategy of establishing a lasting peace based on US interests and principles. As a result, FDR's foreign policy leadership launched a major shift in America's global role that has lasted into the twenty-first century.

Roosevelt's Republican predecessors had intended to exercise leadership in foreign affairs outside of the League of Nations by using America's economic might to promote peace and stability, but their approach was in shambles by the time he took office. Following the 1923 reparations crisis, the US government made substantial loans to ease France's and Germany's financial troubles, negotiated war debt reductions, and monitored the transatlantic flow of private capital that helped recover European businesses. It also negotiated naval-reduction treaties in the Pacific, arranged international guarantees of China's territorial integrity, and persuaded Japan that collaboration with the United States was beneficial for its security and economy. Republican internationalism crumbled as the Great Depression weakened America's economic strength, which it relied on. Without the lifeline of US financing, Europe reverted to the economic turmoil of the immediate postwar period. This increased the widespread appeal of Adolf Hitler's call to reject the Versailles settlement and follow the Nazi path to national redemption in Germany. Japan annexed Manchuria from China in late 1931 as the first step in constructing a self-sufficient empire in East Asia, despite being cut off from American financing, shut out of the US market by new protective tariffs, and denied raw materials when the European powers closed their colonies to foreign commerce.

FDR brought to office his long-held Wilsonian conviction that nations were interdependent in their common need for long-term peace and prosperity, but tempered this with a recognition, based on the 1919 experience, that an international cooperation foreign policy required popular support at home. Seeing Hitler's election as German chancellor as a threat to peace, he warned French ambassador Paul Claudel during pre-inauguration negotiations that the US, Britain, and France should work together to stop Nazi aggression. He also reaffirmed his support for the Stimson Doctrine of non-recognition of Japan's takeover of Chinese territory (adopted by Secretary of State Henry Stimson). However, his internationalist goals were limited when his early measures failed to garner international backing and sparked domestic criticism.

Two months into his presidency, Roosevelt sent a letter to fifty-four heads of state encouraging armaments reduction, non-aggression, and global commerce expansion. This was intended to help the World Disarmament Conference, which is currently taking place in Geneva, as well as the upcoming World Economic Conference in London. It gave FDR a brief international reputation as a leader in the cause of international peace. Concerns in Congress that selective embargoes would drag the US into global conflict caused him to abandon efforts to achieve a resolution forbidding arms sales to aggressor governments, which he saw as necessary for American participation in collective efforts to promote peace. France became increasingly obstinate in refusing Hitler's rearmament demands without a definite assurance of US backing if attacked. On 14 October, the German dictator broke the impasse by removing his country from the Geneva Conference and the League of Nations, convincing Roosevelt to forego further efforts to encourage disarmament. 'In the current European scenario,' he wrote to Presbyterian minister Harry Emerson Fosdick, 'I feel very much as if I were searching for a door in a blank wall.' Only an improvement in the transatlantic situation would "allow us to provide some leadership." In reality, there was no hope of things improving until the United States was participating in the process.

Meanwhile, Roosevelt's fears that Britain and France were attempting to broker a currency exchange rate agreement prompted him to release the 'bombshell' telegram on 3 July, which blew up the London Economic Conference. The war-debt debate then drove a wedge between America and Britain. In late 1933, the United Kingdom offered $460 million in full settlement of Great War loans that had ballooned to $8 billion due to excessive interest rates, more than double the initial value. Rejecting this as deplorable, Roosevelt backed a punitive move suggested by Senator Hiram Johnson (R-California) that barred foreign nations in arrears on their war-debt repayments from marketing bond issues in the United States. Debtor nations had little motivation to pay what they owed because they could no longer make partial repayments. With no possibility of restitution from its own war debtors to meet its American debts, Britain became a defaulter, a significant blow to national dignity. Sir

Ronald Lindsay, its ambassador in Washington, remarked angrily, 'There is something truly sadistic about the way in which American Democracy - or rather Demagogy - acts in a situation like this... to indulge its wrath in a frenzy of cruelty.'

Roosevelt explored alternative ways to advance his internationalist agenda after failing to make headway on the world stage. The United States continued to refuse to recognize the Bolshevik regime that had seized power in Russia in 1917. FDR saw the Soviet Union as a progressive power dedicated to developing a more equitable society at home and combating fascism abroad, and he saw an opportunity for rapprochement. 'Gosh, if I could only talk to one man representing the Russians, I could clear this whole thing out,' he admitted to Henry Morgenthau. With the State Department opposed to Soviet recognition, FDR utilized trusted intermediaries to approach Moscow informally about establishing high-level talks. Meanwhile, he began to garner domestic support by emphasizing the trade benefits of formal recognition. This allowed Soviet Foreign Minister Maxim Litvinov to visit Washington in November 1933 to discuss "unresolved issues." The ensuing accord, negotiated in White House meetings with FDR, terminated America's status as the only notable country that did not recognize the Soviet Union. Normalization of relations did not bring their governments closer together in the 1930s, but it did pave the way for Lend-Lease help to Russia after Hitler's invasion in 1941.

FDR reaped more immediate benefits from a fresh strategy to Latin America, where America's propensity of military intervention throughout the first third of the twentieth century had created resentment of "Yankee imperialism." In an address to the Pan-American Union on April 12, 1933, he declared the United States' commitment to equality and cooperation among Western Hemisphere nations, recognised their independence, and supported the reduction of trade obstacles. This created the groundwork for the Good Neighbour strategy, under which the US sought favorable relations with Latin American nations in order to strengthen hemispheric solidarity in a perilous world and improve trade.

Roosevelt refrained from sending soldiers to quell political unrest in Cuba, which had been virtually America's ward since its independence from Spain in 1898. Following recognition of the conservative nationalist government that came to power in early 1934 with the support of military strongman Fulgencio Batista, the US provided it with a $4 million loan, agreed to a new commercial treaty, and repealed the Platt Amendment of 1903, which enshrined the US right of intervention in Cuban affairs. FDR also honored Herbert Hoover's pledge to end the twenty-year presence of US marines in Haiti, effectively ending American military control of Latin America.

When the US delegation negotiated the resolution of previously contentious issues including sovereignty, trade, and debt repayment at the Pan-American Conference in Montevideo in December 1933, hemispheric cooperation received a further boost. The following summer, Roosevelt gave a personal touch to the rapprochement by visiting Columbia on a holiday cruise, making him the first sitting president to visit South America. Huge throngs gathered to support him on his 12,000-mile sea voyage to Argentina for the Pan-American Conference in late 1936 confirmed the significant improvement in US-Latin American relations. Encouraged by the 'viva la democracia!' chants that greeted his disembarkation, FDR wrote to Ambassador William Dodd in Berlin, 'Those people down there were for me because I have made democracy function and keep abreast of the times, and that as a system of government, it is, therefore, to be preferred to Fascism or Communism.' As Europe's position deteriorated, the Good Neighbour policy permitted the United States' defense preparations to expand hemispheric in scope. The Pan-American Conferences of 1938, 1939, and 1940 all resulted in significant accords about mutual security, neutrality, and economic cooperation.

The dollar's value stabilization in early 1934 spurred Roosevelt to request a reciprocal trade measure permitting him to negotiate bilateral agreements with other nations that allowed mutual adjustments of up to 50% in existing tariffs without the need for

Senate treaty ratification. Secretary of State Cordell Hull, a staunch free trader, believed the increased international trade would lessen the likelihood of war. Roosevelt was more practical, wishing mainly for increased trade among treaty partners. The nineteen bilateral agreements completed by the end of 1939 (including eleven with Latin American republics) would be mostly beneficial to the United republics, as indicated by the nearly tripling of its favorable trade balance since 1934.

The trade agreements signed with Canada in 1935 and with the United Kingdom and France in 1938 were politically significant in displaying the Atlantic powers' solidarity at a time of mounting international crises. The first of them brought an unofficial trade war between the two North American neighbors to an end. Following its adoption, FDR wrote to Canada's long-serving Liberal prime minister, William Mackenzie King, saying, 'In a sense, we both took our political lives into our own hands for a good cause, and I am very delighted to believe that the result has proven so successful.' This marked the beginning of a long-standing cooperation in which the two presidents communicated informally about world matters via correspondence, phone calls, and personal meetings. More broadly, the reciprocal trade program laid the groundwork for the post-World War II multilateral trade liberalization. The tariff negotiating mechanism devised under its auspices provided the paradigm for the General Agreement on Tariffs and Trade, which was signed by 23 countries in 1947.

As FDR was well aware, economic internationalism was insufficient to curb the growing fascist assault. In 1935, Hitler revealed the existence of a German air force and plans to build a 550,000-strong army in violation of the Versailles disarmament clauses, Italian dictator Benito Mussolini launched an East African colonial war, and Japan signaled its Pacific ambitions by demanding naval parity with the United States and Britain. In his 1936 message to Congress, FDR declared, 'A point has been reached where the people of the Americas must take cognizance of growing ill-will, of marked trends towards aggression, of increasing armaments, of shortening tempers -

a situation that has in it many of the elements that lead to the tragedy of general war.' Regardless, the American people overwhelmingly opposed the modest efforts he recommended to keep the peace.

In one of history's ironies, the Supreme Court, which had declared many New Deal domestic policies illegal in 1935-6, ruled in United States v. Curtiss-Wright (1936) that the president was not subject to congressional or judicial restraint as the sole organ in foreign affairs. The case stemmed from a legal challenge to FDR's decision to impose an embargo on arms sales to Chaco War adversaries Bolivia and Paraguay. Cold War presidents would assert their inherent primacy in foreign affairs, citing the sole organ's argument, to assess the nation's best interests overseas. Wary of asserting such authority, Roosevelt decided in the mid-1930s that it was more expedient to placate the overwhelming attitude in Congress and the country that rejected his efforts to fight foreign aggression beyond the western hemisphere. 'For the time being,' noted biographer Robert Dallek, 'he was a foreign policy leader without a following.'

In private, Roosevelt criticized "the very large... school of thought that holds that we can and should withdraw wholly within ourselves and cut off all but the most perfunctory relations with other nations."This diatribe grossly misrepresented the beliefs of those on the other side of the debate on America's world role in the 1930s, which included absolute opposition to America's involvement in another foreign war unless it was attacked; insistence on total rather than selective embargoes on belligerents to ensure that US neutrality was never jeopardized; rejection of collective security and membership in international organizations; and support for military force levels.

Absolute neutrality in foreign conflicts was the principal creed of so-called isolationists, a phrase that became widely used as a derogatory slur only after America entered World War II. Neutralism was most prevalent in the Midwest and Great Plains, and least frequent in the South; it was most prevalent among German Americans, Italian Americans, and Irish Americans; and it was somewhat stronger among women than men. Though it received more support from voters with less formal education than from those with more formal education, a large number of intellectuals and scholars were adamant that the United States not be drawn into another European struggle. For example, eminent historian Charles Beard argued vehemently that America, acting alone or in alliance, lacked the strength to restore peace and democracy to a continent "encrusted in the blood-rust of fifty centuries." Advocates of rigorous neutrality were found among conservatives and liberals in both parties, with the Republican Party being stronger than the Democratic Party.

Popular conviction that US involvement in the Great War had been a mistake strengthened determination not to be drawn into another conflict. Walter Millis best-selling The Road to War, 1914-1917 asserted that America's insistence on defending its neutral right to trade with the belligerents had effectively made it a silent partner to the Anglo-French alliance. Its arguments fuelled demands for new legislation that would preserve America's impartial neutrality through forbidding commerce with any country at war. Advancing a parallel 'merchants-of-death' argument, a Senate special committee investigating the munitions industry, chaired by arch-neutralist Gerald Nye (R-North Dakota), contended that collusion between the Wilson government, weapon-manufacturers and bankers instigated the call to arms of 1917. Another common belief held a cabal of pro-British advisers to blame for misleading Woodrow Wilson into belligerency. In the public mind, accordingly, strict limitation on presidential discretion in foreign affairs was essential to keep America out of another war. This outlook precipitated the defeat in early 1935 of FDR's request for Senate approval of US membership of the World Court, the judicial arm of the League of Nations created to arbitrate international disputes and uphold the Versailles treaty system.

A complacent president did not undertake a public campaign for what he considered a largely symbolic gesture of support for the international rule of law, but he underestimated the widespread hostility to any suggestion of involvement with the League of Nations. Radio priest Charles Coughlin and William Randolph Hearst's newspapers together raised popular agitation to fever pitch with warnings that the American way of life was at risk. Deluded with 40,000 telegrams of opposition and an even larger volume of hostile mail, the Senate fell seven short of the two-thirds majority required for ratification. Never acknowledging his own misjudgement, an exasperated FDR told Senate Majority Leader Joseph Robinson (D-Arkansas) that those voting nay had damaged the cause of peace. '[I]f they ever get to Heaven', he remarked, 'they will be doing a great deal of apologizing for a very long time – that is if God is against war – and I think He is.' Unwilling to risk further defeats, he told Henry Stimson, 'I fear common sense dictates no new method for the time being.'

Neutrality legislation enacted by Congress constituted further setbacks for presidential foreign policy leadership. As tensions between Italy and Ethiopia grew in the spring of 1935, Roosevelt's maneuvers to obtain an arms embargo against aggressor nations aroused suspicion that he was seeking implicit authority to support League of Nations sanctions. Determined to exclude America from implied participation in collective security, the Senate insisted on a bill mandating impartial neutrality. To avoid a prolonged legislative battle that would delay consideration of major domestic measures, including Social Security, Roosevelt settled for a six-month ban on trade in weapons and war materials with all belligerents. When Mussolini's invasion went ahead in October, it steamrolled to victory in a matter of months against an ill-equipped adversary. The president hoped in vain that popular sympathy for the outgunned underdog would induce Congress to grant him discretionary power to invoke embargoes against aggressors when the Neutrality Act came up for renewal. Opponents countered that this would only encourage European dependence on America to stiffen collective security. With his eye on re-election, Roosevelt accepted a compromise that extended the existing law with added provisions banning loans and credits to belligerents until April 1937.

Political difficulties at home early in his second term made FDR loathe to court additional troubles on foreign affairs. Although the neutrality legislation did not prohibit arms sales in the case of internal conflict, Cordell Hull enjoyed a rare moment of influence in counseling the president not to take a stand against congressional approval of a joint resolution extending the embargo to the Civil War precipitated in Spain by General Francisco Franco's fascist uprising against the Republican government.

This brought the United States into line with the Anglo-French viewpoint, but it was a case of three blind mice, not three wise men. While the democracies remained neutral, Germany and Italy fought alongside Franco's rebels as co-belligerents. According to Claude Bowers, America's ambassador in Madrid, the Civil War became "a foreign war of the Fascist Powers against the government of Spain." The embargo restricted Roosevelt's hands for the duration of the war, which concluded in Franco's victory in early 1939. In a rare acknowledgment of error, he told the Cabinet that America had made a "grave mistake" by failing to sell Loyalist Spain "what she needed to fight for her life."

Meanwhile, in May 1937, Congress passed another Neutrality Act, maintaining the mandatory restriction on arms sales and financial assistance to warring countries, as well as preventing Americans from traveling on their passenger ships. It also implemented a 'cash-and-carry' regulation, which required belligerents to pay in cash for non-military goods such as oil and copper and convey them away in their own ships. The Supreme Court squabble rendered Roosevelt a bystander amid legislative negotiations on a law that denied the US any leverage over aggressor states as conflict in Europe and Asia grew closer. Skirmishes between Japanese and Chinese troops on the outskirts of Beijing escalated into a full-scale yet undeclared war only two months after FDR signed it.

To regain control of Manchuria, which was increasingly essential to Japan's economy, Japan launched an invasion of China, capturing the main city, Shanghai, in November 1937, and the capital, Nanking, a month later, where its troops massacred civilians and committed mass rape. While the battle was still in its early phases, Cordell Hull asked President Jimmy Carter to deliver a dramatic statement urging worldwide cooperation in support of peace. FDR agreed to do so on the return leg of his tour to the West on October 5, in Chicago, a neutralist stronghold. It was his most major foreign policy speech since entering office, and it signaled the beginning of a deliberate public push to persuade Americans that increased engagement abroad was a national imperative.

Roosevelt significantly revised the draft provided by the State Department in order to make his argument more compelling. 'The monuments and traditions that have distinguished the advance of civilization towards a state of law, order, and justice are being swept away,' he said, without naming any attacker. Civilians, including women and children, are being cruelly slaughtered with bombs dropped from the sky without a declaration of war and without any warning or explanation.' It was impossible for any nation, including the United States, to "completely isolate itself from economic and political upheavals in the rest of the world, particularly when such upheavals appear to be spreading rather than declining." The most notable paragraph of the address, written by the president himself, urged for action to combat the "epidemic of global lawlessness" in order to prevent "the contagion of war." To that purpose, he drew a comparison with the establishment of a 'quarantine' to prevent the spread of a contagious bodily ailment. 'The will for peace on the part of peace-loving nations must express itself so that nations that may be tempted to breach their agreements and the rights of others will desist from such a course,' Roosevelt declared.

The message drew a largely positive reception from the press and public opinion, owing to popular outrage over Japanese crimes in China and the destruction of the Spanish village of Guernica by German warplanes, but there was little support for follow-up measures. Concerned that Roosevelt's 'quarantine the aggressors' words had gone too far, Cordell Hull and Democratic leaders in Congress withheld public backing. The speech, according to Hull, delayed "for at least six months our constant educational campaign aimed at creating and strengthening public opinion toward international cooperation." Roosevelt himself backed down from its implications the next day, rejecting any intention to impose economic punishment on aggressors. He claimed that the quarantine speech 'is an attitude, and it does not specify a program, but it says we are looking for a program'. Nonetheless, its message established the groundwork for his four-year rhetorical campaign to convince the public that the US had a critical stake in preserving a world ruled by rules and moral principles of civilization rather than unbridled power politics. 'I truly feel,' he told Colonel Edward House, an old Wilsonian, 'that as time passes, we can gradually but steadily make people realize that war will be a greater risk to us if we close all the doors and windows than if we walk out in the street and use our influence to quell the riot.

Two months later, Japan violated US neutrality by sinking the US gunboat Panay on the Yangtze River as it assisted Americans escaping the besieged city of Nanking. In response to an episode that emphasized his warnings about international lawlessness, Roosevelt sought apologies, compensation, and guarantees against future attacks, and briefly pondered punitive actions. For supporters of strict neutrality, the Panay event highlighted the hazards of America being involved in foreign strife. It spurred their campaign to gain a constitutional amendment requiring a majority vote in a national referendum before a declaration of war by Congress could take effect, except in cases of attack or danger of attack. The president's role in its defeat demonstrated that his clout in the national discussion about neutrality was finally growing.

The concept of deciding war or peace through popular vote has a long history, but it has never gained widespread acceptance. Assuming leadership of the effort in 1935, Representative Louis Ludlow (D-Indiana) worked hard in Congress to garner support for a referendum amendment to the Constitution. With the House Judiciary Committee considering his motion, he was 13 signatures short of the 218 required for a floor vote on its discharge when the Panay sank. The adoption of the amendment, according to Roosevelt and Hull, would 'indicate to the world that the nation no longer trusted the Administration to conduct its foreign affairs' and 'would serve notice on the aggressor nations that they could take any action anywhere in the world... with little if any likelihood of any concrete reaction from Washington'. The president appointed to Democratic National Committee Chairman James Farley the task of lining up votes against discharge using every political and patronage resource at his disposal. He also warned Speaker William Bankhead (D-Alabama) that the amendment "would cripple any President's conduct of our foreign relations." During the discharge debate on 10 January 1938, the Speaker stepped down from the podium to give a dramatic reading from the floor of the letter from "our Commander in Chief, a man who loves peace as passionately and devotedly as any man who breathes the air of God in America this day or anywhere else in the world." Less than 30 minutes later, the House voted 209 to 188 against the release.

Over the Roosevelt administration's opposition, the amendment had no chance of receiving the needed two-thirds majority in both houses of Congress to be sent to the states for ratification. Nonetheless, the battle for its release emboldened supporters of more global engagement, including Northeastern business and political elites, the internationalist wings of both major parties, veterans' organizations, and most of the metropolitan press. As a result, Henry Stimson regarded the Ludlow amendment as "the pinnacle of the American people's pre-war deception."

At this point, FDR was still under the impression that international civilization was fundamentally healthy. He was confident that the overwhelming presence of friendly nations would assure the success of coordinated efforts to restrain a small number of aggressors. As he stated in his 'quarantine' talk, 'the peace, freedom, and security of ninety percent of the world's population is being imperiled by the remaining ten percent, who are threatening the breakdown of all international order and law.' According to him, the 'ninety percent' who wish to live in peace 'can and must find some way to make their will prevail'. Such reasoning underpinned his proposal, made in various incarnations from 1936 to 1938, for an international conference to define norms for world peace, with the goal of gaining domestic support for collaboration with states that backed ideas championed by the US.

In January 1938, Roosevelt adopted Under Secretary of State Sumner Welles' plan for a conference in Washington to discuss international behavior guidelines. He made covert overtures seeking British support for a meeting of representatives from small states - Belgium, Hungary, the Netherlands, Sweden, Switzerland, Turkey, Yugoslavia, and three (yet unnamed) Latin American republics - to develop a protocol for promotion to other nations in collaboration with the US. This was the tentative start of his tacit alliance' with Britain, a term coined by arch-neutralist Senator William Borah (R-Idaho) in early 1938, which would grow in substance and significance in opposition to Nazi Germany over the next three years.

To Prime Minister Neville Chamberlain, the idea for the small-nation conference was a 'preposterous effusion' that 'risked cutting across our efforts' at 'a measure of appeasement' of Germany and Italy. His refusal to back Roosevelt's initiative effectively killed it, at cost of the resignation of Foreign Secretary Anthony Eden, who considered Anglo-American cooperation essential to restrain the dictators. A decade later Winston Churchill recalled his 'breathless amazement' that his predecessor had discarded 'the last frail chance to save the world from tyranny otherwise than by war' through waving away 'the proffered hand stretched out across the Atlantic'. In truth, Chamberlain had no reason to believe that the prospective international conference would rein in Hitler or even that it represented a real change in American policy, since its proposal was accompanied by a declaration of continued intent to abstain from involvement in European affairs. William Bullitt, ambassador to France, sent Roosevelt a blunt but accurate assessment of its utility: 'It would be as if in the palmiest days of Al Capone, you had summoned a national conference of psychoanalysts to Washington to discuss the psychological causes of crime.'

The events of 1938 disabused Roosevelt of his optimism about the basic well-being of international society. Unbeknown to him, Hitler had informed his senior military and political officials in a meeting at the Reich Chancellery on 5 November 1937 that Germany's need for territorial and economic expansion could only be attained through force. In a two-hour exposition, he outlined his war plans and assessed the likely responses of other European powers and Japan (he paid no heed to the United States). To his mind, war had to come within the next few years, possibly as early as 1938 and no later than 1945, for Germany to exploit its current superiority in armaments. Despite his generals' doubts about risking conflict with Britain and France, Hitler took the first step to war by annexing Austria through the Anschluss of March 1938. His next foray targeted Czechoslovakia's largely German-speaking Sudeten region in the west of the country. War seemingly loomed with Britain and France, but their governments resolved to settle the crisis through appeasement. After two meetings with Hitler in which he met every concession with further demands, Neville Chamberlain and French premier Edouard Daladier agreed on the immediate incorporation of Sudetenland into Germany in a third conference at Munich on 29 September 1938. The settlement bought Britain and France a year to prepare for eventual war, which Hitler had wanted over Czechoslovakia.

FDR was initially appalled to learn that Britain and France aimed to appease Hitler's demand for Czech territory, telling the Cabinet that their leaders would 'wash the blood of Judas Iscariot from their hands'. Nevertheless, he was unwilling to stiffen Anglo-French resolve with promises of American support. A plea to all the parties to preserve peace omitted any offer of help in resolving the dispute and asserted, for good measure, that America had 'no political entanglements'. On hearing that Chamberlain was heading to Munich for a third effort to find a settlement, Roosevelt sent the prime minister a two-word telegram, 'Good man'.

Despite his disengagement from its outcome, Munich constituted a turning point in FDR's foreign policy leadership. At a White House meeting of military advisers and trusted confidantes, he remarked that 'the recrudescence of German power . . .had completely reoriented our own international relations', putting America itself at risk of attack from across the Atlantic. The Kristallnacht pogrom of 9–10 November 1938, Nazi-organized attacks on Jews, their homes, property and synagogues, and the German state's confiscation of all Jewish assets reinforced his conviction that Hitler would never respect international norms. In a brief public statement at his 15 November press conference, he remarked, 'I myself could scarcely believe that such things could occur in a twentieth century civilization.' In response, Roosevelt instructed the State Department to summon home the American ambassador to Berlin for 'report and consultation', a recall that proved permanent.

FDR's growing anxiety about the fascist menace of worldwide lawlessness confirmed his long-held belief that State Department officials, notably those in the Division of Eastern European Affairs, supported Hitler as a counter-balance to the Soviet Union. Since becoming President, he has effectively served as his own Secretary of State, deferring to Cordell Hull on trade and economic diplomacy but mostly bypassing him on political affairs. Assuming increasing policymaking authority after Munich, he worked more closely with Under Secretary of State Sumner Welles, a long-standing friend and fellow Groton, who reinforced the president's determination to play a more active role in world affairs following his appointment in 1937. Roosevelt maintained his practice of depending on personnel he had selected to ambassadorial posts, whose loyalty were to him rather than the State Department, for knowledge on foreign matters. Claude Bowers in Madrid, William Bullitt in Paris, Joseph Davies in Moscow (later Brussels), William Dodd in Berlin, and Joseph Grew in Tokyo were among them, but not Joseph Kennedy, an arch-appeaser in his new job as Ambassador to the United Kingdom.

Despite his mounting fury, Roosevelt expected other countries to shoulder the burden of Hitler's resistance. When he saw Lord Lothian in February 1939, he 'went furious right through' when he was told that America should become the primary guardian of Anglo-Saxon civilization. 'What the British need today,' he wrote to a friend, 'is a good stiff grog, inspiring not only the desire to defend civilization, but also the continuing belief that they can accomplish it.' Air power was the 'grog' he had in mind. Immediately following Munich, Roosevelt obtained information from William Bullitt suggesting Anglo-French inadequacy in this area was primarily to blame for their departure from Czechoslovakia. This convinced him that the US should dramatically boost its own aircraft production, mostly for purchase by Britain and France, in order to establish aerial forces capable of overpowering Hitler or, in the event of war, destroying him without America becoming belligerent. During a five-day retreat to Hyde Park in mid-October 1938, the president discussed his aircraft production targets with Bullitt, Treasury Secretary Henry Morgenthau, and work-relief supremo Harry Hopkins. Jean Monnet, the Daladier government's agent responsible for obtaining FDR's pledge to supply France with warplanes, and Arthur Murray, a long-standing British anti-appeasement figure, were both present. According to Murray's notes of their meetings, Roosevelt gave him permission to advise Chamberlain that if war broke out with Germany, he would have "the industrial resources of the American nation behind him." To avoid neutrality regulations, their supply would come in the form of partially finished materials, enough to manufacture an additional 20,000-30,000 warplanes.

This was a speculative figure that ignored productive capacity constraints, the needs of the US armed forces, and domestic political realities. The $500 million supplemental defense budget submitted to Congress in January 1939 requested $180 million for the production of only 3,000 combat planes, with the remainder designated for other military uses. After falling short on quantity, FDR sought to compensate by improving the quality of aircraft offered for sale. Jean Monnet, who was given the authority to purchase 1,000 US warplanes, discovered that existing models did not match French specifications. Despite the War Department's reservations, Roosevelt insisted on the French inspecting and purchasing three experimental planes that were not yet in production: the Curtiss P-40 fighter, the Martin 167 bomber, and the Douglas DB-7 bomber. 'If your theory [is] that England and France are our first line of defense... let's either give them the good stuff or tell them to go home, but don't give some stuff that the minute it goes up in the air it will be shot down,' said Henry Morgenthau, acting as point man to expedite the buying spree.

Hopes of keeping the purchases secret were dashed when a Douglas bomber carrying a French official crashed in California on January 23, 1939. When called before the Senate Military Affairs Committee, Morgenthau justified foreign sales as advantageous to the development costs of the new planes, while Secretary of War Harry Woodring maintained that they jeopardized Army Air Force procurement. To avoid a full-fledged probe, Roosevelt invited the entire committee to a private briefing at the White House on January 31. During his first two terms in office, this was his most candid foreign policy declaration before legislators. He declared his desire to 'avoid it by peaceful means' after warning that Germany, Italy, and Japan were pursuing a "policy of world domination." In this endeavor, America's "first line of defense" extended well beyond its borders. A line of islands in the Pacific held the key to assuring that US naval and air power could resist Japanese expansion. To restrain Germany and Italy in Europe, the 'continued autonomous existence' of twenty nations was critical. It was in America's best interests to assist Britain and France in acquiring the necessary air strength. 'There would not have been any Munich' if their capability had been twice what it was in 1938. America would mitigate the threat of aggressor states by selling its best jets to Britain and France without having to go to war. 'About the last thing this country should ever do,' Roosevelt informed his audience, 'is send an army to Europe again.'

To the president's chagrin, a committee member leaked to the press anonymously that he had declared America's borders to be on the Rhine, words he never used. Other participants said that Roosevelt's categorization of this assertion as a "deliberate lie" in a press conference encouraged others to reveal that his words left little question that he meant to back Anglo-French rearmament regardless of neutrality law. Standing steadfast, FDR used his 17 February press conference to inform reporters and, via them, the public that this was important for America's security. A Gallup poll conducted two weeks following his discussion with the committee revealed that 69% of respondents supported doing everything short of war to assist Britain and France in a battle with Germany and Italy.

When Germany conquered what remained of Czechoslovakia, any chance that Roosevelt's more open support for Anglo-French rearmament would discourage Nazi aggression vanished. Within weeks, the British government declared its commitment to defending Poland, which was widely assumed to be Hitler's next objective. The abandoning of appeasement paved the way for a general European conflict. In communications conveyed to Hitler and Mussolini on April 14, Roosevelt made his final public appeal for peace. His seven-page message to the German dictator requested a ten-year commitment that he would not attack or invade the land of the thirty-one specified European and Middle Eastern states. In exchange, the US would take part in an international conference to consider ways to reduce 'the heavy burden of weapons' and open up international trade to all countries on equal terms.

Infuriated that Roosevelt had released the communication before its official reception in Berlin, Hitler first considered it beneath his dignity to respond to "such a contemptible creature." The positive reaction it received throughout most of Europe, including Germany, prompted a response in the shape of a two-and-a-half-hour speech to the Reichstag that mocked the president's idea. 'A horrific flogging of Roosevelt,' Nazi propaganda minister Joseph Goebbels exclaimed. 'That truly smacks him in the face... Anyone who publicly criticizes the Fuhrer receives his comeuppance...In comparison, what a pigmy Roosevelt is.' Some domestic critics were also pleased that FDR "put his chin out and... got a resounding whack on it," as Senator Hiram Johnson phrased it.

Despite this, FDR's initiative had significant consequences for Hitler's strategic calculation. As historian Ian Kershaw observed, the Nazi leader could have no illusions that 'whatever the appearances of neutrality, the United States now had to be regarded as essentially a hostile power'. Hitherto he had paid little attention to a distant country seemingly so weakened by economic crisis that it lacked both the will and the military capability to become involved in European affairs. His Nazi eugenics also impelled him to disdain FDR personally as the crippled leader of a mongrel nation. Seeing the United States anew as a potential threat rather than an irrelevance, Hitler sought to ensure its neutrality in his imminent war with Britain and France. Though not yet precisely formulated, a basic assumption took root in his geopolitical thinking that conflict with America should be deferred until Germany dominated Europe and possessed a mighty fleet capable of contesting control of the seas.

Holding no illusions that the fascist dictators would respond positively, FDR had really aimed his message at the American people. As he told Mackenzie King, 'If we are turned down, the issue becomes clearer and public opinion in your country and mine will be helped.' He hoped to generate support for arms-embargo repeal in order to continue supplying the European democracies with weapons when they were at war with Germany. Popular approval for doing so declined from its high point following his meeting with the Senate Armed Services Committee to 57 per cent in April and continued falling to the point that opposition to repeal enjoyed majority support in August. By contrast, public support for enlarging America's own military forces ran between 80 and 90 per cent throughout 1939, with some two-thirds of poll respondents declaring willingness to pay higher taxes if needed.

The survey returns did not deter Roosevelt from seeking to rescind the arms embargo. Largely uninvolved in earlier struggles over neutrality legislation, he lobbied behind the scenes and eventually out in the open in support of allowing weapons sales to belligerents on a cash-and-carry basis, terms obviously advantageous to the democracies because of Britain's naval supremacy. Neither presidential exhortation nor the public-relations success of the British royal visit of King George VI and Queen Elizabeth to the United States in early June swayed congressional hearts and minds. Thanks to Democratic defections, the House of Representatives upheld the current law by a vote of 200 to 188 on 30 June, while the Senate Foreign Relations Committee voted 12 to 11 to defer consideration of the amendment until the next congressional session. Grasping at straws, FDR invited a bipartisan group of senators to the White House on 18 July to ask their support for revision before the chamber recessed. With William Borah to the fore, GOP attendees expressed skepticism that war was imminent and questioned Hitler's readiness to fight. Even if a repeal bill emerged from committee, it was evident that a Republican filibuster would talk it to death on the chamber floor. Accepting that he could do no more for now, Roosevelt laid the foundations for another effort when war broke out in Europe with some strong statements that the Senate had made this eventuality more likely. Most notably, he asserted at his press conference of 21 July that it had 'accepted the responsibility of saying to the Executive Branch of the Government, "There is nothing further you can do to avert war"'.

Once the Nazi-Soviet non-aggression pact of 23 August 1939 safeguarded Germany's eastern flank, Hitler launched the invasion of Poland on 1 September, precipitating the Anglo-French declarations of war two days later. On the evening of 3 September, FDR delivered a Fireside Chat in which he declared, 'This nation will remain a neutral nation, but I cannot ask that every American remain neutral in thought as well. Even a neutral has a right to take account of facts. Even a neutral cannot be asked to close his mind or his conscience.' This statement was markedly different from Woodrow Wilson's plea for Americans to be 'impartial in thought as well as in action' at the outbreak of the Great War. Over the next two months, opinion polls showed that Americans by margins of four-to-one favored an Allied victory, while some three-fifths wanted to do everything possible to help bring that about 'short of going to war ourselves'.

FDR's new issue was to assist Britain and France without generating popular fear that he was attempting to turn America into a belligerent. The relaunch of the campaign to lift the arms embargo was a wonderful example of his juggling act. On September 21,

Roosevelt called a special session of Congress and said that putting all trade with belligerents on a cash-and-carry basis was the best way to keep the country neutral. 'Let no organization claim the unique name of "peace bloc," he said. 'We're all a part of it.' Following that, he delegated legislative work to Democratic leaders in Congress, recruited Republican sympathizers to lobby for the bill (notably, 1936 presidential running mates Alfred Landon and Frank Knox), and encouraged the formation of the Nonpartisan Committee for Peace Through the Revision of the Neutrality Act to garner popular support. 'I am practically literally walking on eggs,' FDR said to Lord Tweedsmuir, Governor-General of Canada, 'at the present saying nothing, seeing nothing, and hearing nothing.' In early November, he was rewarded with Senate majorities of 55 to 24 and House majorities of 243 to 181 for repealing the arms embargo.

The measure was lauded by Neville Chamberlain as providing the Allies access to "the greatest storehouse of supplies in the world," but it was more a case of poorhouse fair. According to the British Treasury, the cash-and-carry rule, along with the modified neutrality legislation's continuous prohibition on loans to belligerents, made America a "limited marginal source of war supplies." To preserve the United Kingdom's gold and dollar reserves for a lengthy war, it initially prioritized purchasing food and raw materials over weaponry. Despite the fact that the US government and people were much more friendly to Britain and France in 1939-40 than in 1914-17, America's productive force was far less helpful to their cause in the early stages of World War II than it had been in the Great War.

With Germany reserving offensive operations in Western Europe for the duration of the eight-month charade, US leaders and public opinion shared the assumption of eventual Allied victory. Hitler's blitzkrieg, a new type of warfare that incorporated tanks, air power, artillery, and motorized infantry into a plan of quick mobility and maximizing battlefield opportunity, put an end to such complacency. In less than two months, his armies had taken control of Norway, Denmark, the Netherlands, and Belgium, prompting France to call for peace on June 22. The majority of Americans were convinced that a victorious Germany would attack the United States.

As France fell, Roosevelt used an address at the University of Virginia to declare a response to Hitler's success: 'We will extend to the opponents of force the material resources of this nation; and, at the same time, we will harness and speed up the use of those resources in order that we ourselves... may have equipment and training equal to the task of any emergency and every defense.' The second component of the approach proved simple to implement, but at considerable expense to the first. By the end of 1940, Congress had increased the defense budget to five times its pre-Blitzkrieg level, but the Walsh amendment to the Naval Expansion Act required the relevant service chief to certify that the equipment was not essential to America's defense. The Selective Training and Service Act of 1940, passed by large majorities in Congress in September, was the first peacetime conscription in American history, requiring men aged twenty-one to thirty-five to register with local draft boards (later extended to all eighteen to forty-five-year-olds when the United States entered the war), but limited their service to the western hemisphere or American possessions elsewhere. Meanwhile, the public has repeatedly approved the sale of airplanes and other weapons to Britain as long as it does not jeopardize America's own defense effort.

In these conditions, Roosevelt maneuvered to assist Britain while staying ahead of home opinion. He effectively ordered military chiefs to classify items as "surplus," which was required for their legal release, and he was able to get half-a-million Enfield rifles, 35,000 machine guns, 500 field guns, and ammunition shipped to Britain to replace what had been left behind during the Dunkirk evacuation. FDR urged Henry Morgenthau, who was in charge of the endeavor, to 'give it an extra push every morning and every night until it is on the ships.' Major Walter Bedell Smith, one of Army Chief of Staff George Marshall's top aides, expressed dismay at the scale of the weapons transfer, saying, '[I]f we were required to mobilize after having released guns necessary for this mobilization and were found to be short of artillery materiel, everyone who was a party to the deal might hope to be found hanging from a lamp post.' Even so, the president had to direct a reluctant Secretary of War, Harry Woodring, to authorize the cargo. In November, Roosevelt authorized the supply of six B-174 Flying Fortresses to the United Kingdom so that it could bomb Germany's cities while its own were subjected to the Luftwaffe's Blitz. Despite the fact that the US now had less than fifty bombers in service, the transfer was made possible by legal maneuvering that declared the planes non-essential for homeland defense due to their planned replacement by B-24 Liberators, which were not yet on the production line.

The most high-profile arms shipment of 1940 were fifty First World War destroyers, which Prime Minister Winston Churchill, who had succeeded Chamberlain on May 10, had urgently sought in order to oppose a presumably imminent German invasion. In reality, the major objective of the ancient ships, which would take months to repair for modern warfare, was to raise British morale and warn Hitler against putting US neutrality at risk. Nonetheless, FDR waited until he obtained legal advice that congressional approval was unnecessary if the transfer strengthened America's defenses. This need was accomplished by exchanging the destroyers for Britain's gift of two naval facilities in Newfoundland and Bermuda, the lease of further bases in the West Indies for ninety-nine years, and a promise never to surrender or scuttle its fleet if beaten by Germany. In a statement to Congress on September 3, Roosevelt said, "This is the most important action in the reinforcement of our national defense since the Louisiana Purchase." The importance of these security outposts to the Western Hemisphere is incalculable.' Hitler postponed his planned invasion two weeks later due to the Royal Air Force's victory in the Battle of Britain. The destroyers, only nine of which were in British hands by the end of 1940, had little role in Britain's salvation, but their significance for the more open Anglo-American alliance was enormous.

Within a few months, the destroyer contract appeared to be a drop in the bucket as FDR increased his efforts to keep a cash-strapped

Britain in the war. On his way back from meetings in London on November 23, the new UK ambassador, Lord Lothian, told journalists awaiting him at LaGuardia Airport, 'Well, boys, Britain's broke; it's your money we want.' This frank declaration focused American attention on the situation of a country with substantial assets in pound reserves but just enough gold and dollar balances to pay for existing military requirements. 'We are going to pay for the war from now on, aren't we?' said Secretary of the Navy Frank Knox at a Treasury briefing to put military leaders in the picture. He responded to his own question on behalf of everyone present: 'Got to. There is no other option.' Roosevelt was now forced to find a way around the prohibition on lending to belligerents as well as the cash-and-carry requirements of the most recent neutrality act. In early December, he left Washington for a twelve-day Caribbean trip on the USS Tuscaloosa to ponder things through.

The loss of over 900,000 tons of commerce shipping in the last three months, primarily due to U-boat strikes, meant that Britain could 'fall by the way'. The decision for 1941 'lies upon the seas' since convoys of American trade ships escorted by US Navy escorts were the only hope of preserving the Atlantic lifeline. This would still leave Britain's financial crisis unresolved. 'The day is approaching,' Churchill warned, 'when we shall no longer be able to pay cash for shipping and other supplies.' After outlining his country's weaknesses in plain words, the prime minister placed himself in the hands of the president to find a solution that would not leave Britain'stripped to the bone from the forced disposal of its saleable assets in order to win a war fought to rescue civilization. His goal was that "ways and means will be found" that "future generations on both sides of the Atlantic will approve and admire."

According to Harry Hopkins, who was traveling with FDR at the time, the president sat for hours on the Tuscaloosa's deck during the next two days digesting Churchill's message. Then, with the help of this most trusted adviser, he "came out with it - the whole program." The fundamental concept for what became known as 'Lend-Lease,' a term invented by the press, had now given shape. FDR had worked out a method to carry out this operation lawfully by the time he returned to Washington. On December 17, he outlined a plan to 'get away from a dollar sign... and say to England "we will give you the guns and ships that you need, provided that when the war is over you will return to us in kind the guns and ships we have loaned to you, or you will return to us the ships repaired and pay us, always in kind, to make up the depreciation"'. For the Treasury Secretary, Roosevelt's acute sense of 'trade and intuition' answered the public's desire to assist Britain without the suspect baggage of loan funding that was supposed to have led the country into the Great War.

In his news conference that afternoon, FDR announced the Lend-Lease concept. He told reporters that the success of the United Kingdom in defending itself was the 'best immediate protection of the United States.' As domestic military manufacturing reaches new heights, it is considerably better for the UK to employ America's surplus munitions 'than if they were held in storage here'. Roosevelt nailed the essence of Lend-Lease in an appealing analogy that combined reason and emotion in a masterclass in political salesmanship. It was a matter of friendly aid to the British, equivalent to lending a neighbor a garden hose to put out a fire in his home and expecting it to be returned or replaced once the fire was extinguished. According to historian Warren Kimball, the genius of FDR's Lend-Lease policy was that it was "a give-away program that did not look like one."

On December 29, 1940, Roosevelt delivered a Fireside Chat to over three-quarters of adult Americans as well as listeners in portions of Europe and the Far East, the greatest radio audience in history. America's task, he declared, would be to produce vast quantities of weaponry, some of which would be used to boost homeland defense and some of which would be sent abroad to supply Britain and other countries fighting aggression, an allocation the US government would make based on expert military advice on overall necessity. 'We must be democracy's great arsenal,' he declared. 'This is an emergency as serious as war itself for us. We must approach our mission with the same determination, sense of urgency, patriotism, and sacrifice as we would if we were at war.'

A week later, in his State of the Union Address, FDR declared that he would send a Lend-Lease measure to Congress. House supporters skillfully tagged the bill with the patriotic number and title, 'H.R. 1776: A Bill further to Promote the Defense of the United States.' Despite Roosevelt's brilliant use of the presidential podium to pave the way, the legislation was met with strong opposition from strict neutralists, peace groups, and the America First organization, which was formed in the aftermath of the destroyers-for-bases deal to advocate for the building of home defenses first and foremost, and featured famed aviator Charles Lindbergh as its main spokesman.

FDR and his allies increasingly depicted their opponents as appeasers or unwitting dupes of the dictators rather than address valid questions that they raised about America's national interest, the limits of its power, the fiscal costs of Lend-Lease, the likelihood that the programme would eventually make America a belligerent and whether Hitler, even if victorious in Europe, would attack a securely defended United States. Seeing Lindbergh and other opposition luminaries as tantamount to enemies of the republic, the president authorized the Federal Bureau of Investigation to tap their telephones and open their mail. FDR also worked behind the scenes to outmaneuver his critics through more orthodox political means. He persuaded Joseph Kennedy, effectively sacked from his London ambassadorship for doubting Britain's survival, to desist from attacking Lend-Lease when testifying at the invitation of its congressional opponents in House hearings on the bill. Through the good offices of Henry Stimson, formerly Wendell Willkie's lawyer, he also got the 1940 Republican standard-bearer to avow his wholehearted support for Lend-Lease as necessary for Britain's survival when testifying before the Senate Foreign Relations Committee.

Approved by huge majorities in both chambers of Congress, the Lend-Lease legislation went for FDR's signature on 11 March. Nevertheless the opposition had secured important amendments, most notably the prohibition on US Navy convoying of war supplies across the Atlantic. To Churchill's consternation, Roosevelt also agreed that the UK should use its remaining dollar reserves to finance the capital costs of the plant expansion required to manufacture Lend-Lease materials. The Reconstruction Finance Corporation eventually arranged loans to cover this but not before Britain was nearly bled dry through liquidation of its US stock securities. On Lend-Lease's enactment, The New York Times editorialized approvingly that it marked 'the day when the United States ended the great retreat which began with the Senate rejection of the Treaty of Versailles and the League of Nations. The effort to find security in isolation has failed.' Congress appropriated a staggering $7 billion to finance the first shipments of aid to Britain, to be followed by requisitions totalling $13.7 billion for America's own defense needs in calendar 1941. As a share of gross national product, defense outlays rose from 1.4 per cent in 1939 to 11.2 per cent in 1941, while Army personnel rose from 190,000 to 1,500,000.

To the frustration of Henry Stimson, Frank Knox, Henry Morgenthau and Harold Ickes, the strongest voices of intervention in the administration, Roosevelt remained heedful of popular opposition to America joining the war. 'I am not willing to fire the first shot', he told the Cabinet in May. To the so-called all-outers, the president appeared to be looking for an incident that would justify a retaliatory belligerency rather than educating Americans that their involvement in the war was essential for Germany's defeat. 'The President has not aroused the country; has not really sounded the bell . . . does not furnish the motive power that is required', an exasperated Ickes wrote in his diary. When Hitler invaded Russia, Stimson and Knox urged FDR in vain to order the US Navy to protect merchant vessels supplying Britain, an initiative they deemed certain to get America into the war at an opportune moment of Germany's preoccupations in the east. Instead, FDR appeared to think that the new front diminished the need for America to become a formal belligerent.

Whatever the geostrategic case for intervention in the summer of 1941, Roosevelt was being politically astute in not rushing into belligerency. The American people may not have rallied round the flag so enthusiastically if the United States had not come under attack. Holding sole authority to declare war, the House of Representatives may not have done so in the absence of clear provocation. In August, it approved extension of the Selective Service draft for a further fifteen months by just one vote. In reality, of course, Lend-Lease had already consigned America's neutrality to the dustbin of history in establishing a common-law alliance with Britain dedicated to the defeat of Nazi Germany. In the months following its launch, the president took a number of initiatives that moved his country closer to a formal state of war.

FDR extended America's coastline security zone into the mid-Atlantic in early April, ordering US warships to patrol the entire area and authorizing them to notify the British of any sightings of German ships or airplanes. Simultaneously, he declared that American forces would occupy Greenland, a Danish region vulnerable to German takeover. In order to justify this remote area, he declared it to be in the western hemisphere and so subject to the Monroe Doctrine's prohibition on European action. He used the same justification in June to send 4,000 marines to Iceland. Three months later, FDR used an alleged U-boat attack on the US destroyer Greer in the North Atlantic zone of security to push the country to the verge of war. Roosevelt proceeded on the radio to declare what became known as the'shoot-on-sight' policy, claiming the cruiser was an innocent victim of wanton assault when, in fact, it was transmitting the submarine's position to a British aircraft. He referred to the U-boats as "the rattlesnakes of the Atlantic," and stated that any German or Italian ships entering America's security zone would be attacked by US warships and aviation.

It was only a matter of time until both sides started shooting at each other. On October 17, a U-boat struck the US destroyer Kearny, killing eleven sailors and forcing its evacuation to Iceland. In response, Roosevelt gave an unusually combative declaration emphasizing America's willingness to fight Nazi Germany. 'The forward march of Hitler and Hitlerism can and will be stopped,' he said. 'To put it clearly, we have vowed to pull our own oar in the defeat of Hitlerism.' Instead of requesting a declaration of war from Congress, he asked for power to equip American commerce ships and allow them to enter battle zones. By approving this, the legislature effectively invalidated the neutrality legislation's 'carry' restrictions, consigning them to history as Lend-Lease had done for the 'cash' requirements.

As a result of the struggle with Japan, America eventually became hostile. Beginning with Plan Dog, military planners anticipated conflict with Hitler but took a defensive posture in the Pacific to avert a two-ocean war. A week before the attack on Pearl Harbor, Army and Navy chiefs George Marshall and Harold Stark advised FDR that 'an unlimited offensive war against Japan should not be undertaken, because such a war would greatly weaken the combined effort in the Atlantic against Germany, the most dangerous enemy.' In their opinion, it was preferable to make political concessions to Tokyo in order to prevent open conflict. Rather than disregarding their counsel, Roosevelt endeavored to maintain peace in the face of Japan's provocations in attempting territorial expansion in East Asia, but he could not allow a rival to gain dominance in the Pacific.

Unlike his verbal attacks on Hitler, Roosevelt did not launch a public effort to warn Americans about Japan's threat to international civilization. His contacts with the Tokyo government were driven by geopolitics rather than geomorality. Germany's blitzkrieg success in the mid-1940s fueled its ambitions for East Asian conquest. To restrict such ambition, Roosevelt took advantage of Japan's reliance on US imports for vital resources. He put an embargo on premium-grade scrap iron and high-octane aviation fuel supplies on July 26, 1940, but this did not prevent Japan from landing soldiers in Northern Indo-China in late September. Following that, it signed the Tripartite Pact with Germany and Italy, which committed the Axis powers to mutual aid if attacked by a state not currently involved in the European or Sino-Japanese hostilities. This was an obvious attempt to scare America into staying neutral in order to avoid a two-ocean conflict.

For the next twelve months, Tokyo and Washington engaged in a series of escalations aimed at achieving their respective goals while avoiding actual conflict. In reaction to the invasion of Southern Indo-China in July 1941, Roosevelt declared an instant ban on all Japanese assets in the US, but allowed continued oil exports if cleared by a special committee empowered to unblock payments for them. In actuality, this amounted to a de facto oil embargo because the new committee, led by Assistant Secretary of State Dean Acheson, refused to release any holdings. It is debatable whether FDR was complicit in this severe approach in order to sow doubt in Japanese minds, or whether second-tier officials took advantage of the opportunity to impose their hardline opinions. There is no doubt, however, that Roosevelt desired to "slip the noose around Japan's neck and give it a jerk now and then," as he informed the Cabinet.

Nonetheless, FDR remained optimistic that these attempts would not lead to war with Japan. 'It is vitally important for Atlantic control for us to help sustain peace in the Pacific,' he warned Harold Ickes in July 1941. I just don't have enough Navy to go around, and every incident in the Pacific means fewer ships in the Atlantic.' Notably, he handed responsibilities for negotiations with the Japanese government to Cordell Hull while focusing on the more important European theater of war. In fact, by midyear, Japanese authorities had concluded that conflict with America was unavoidable if their country was to increase its strength and affluence through East Asian expansion. They hoped to provoke this before the US increased its troop levels in the Pacific. 'If, for the sake of a short peace, we were today to concede one step towards the United States by a partial retreat from state policy, the strengthening of America's military position will lead to it demanding subsequent retreats of ten steps, then a hundred,' warned an Army General Staff report. Ultimately, the Empire will be forced to do whatever the US wants it to do.'

In November, a new cabinet led by General Hideki Tojo decided on a final diplomatic initiative, which would be followed by the start of military operations if it failed, as expected. In essence, Japan requested free rein in China and the lifting of US economic sanctions in exchange for refraining from future military activities in Southeast Asia. There was no way America would consent to this. FDR pondered counter-offering, but reports of a massive Japanese fleet moving southward put an end to his readiness to deal. Furious at what he saw as Tokyo's ill faith, he endorsed Cordell Hull's severe peace plan, which called for the departure of Japanese soldiers from China and Indo-China. The Imperial Conference of 1 December, seeing this as an insulting ultimatum, agreed to commence planned military operations against 'the immensely conceited, arrogant, and disrespectful' United States.

This gave the go-ahead for the surprise attack on Pearl Harbor on December 7, 1941, without a prior declaration of war. During what aide Samuel Rosenman called "one of the busiest and most turbulent days of his life," crammed with meetings and constant news updates from the Pacific, Roosevelt found time to compose the war speech he would deliver to Congress the next day. To obtain maximum legislative support, the president refused Henry Stimson's request to include Germany and Italy in his declaration of war. He also overruled Cordell Hull's request for a thorough examination of the conditions that led to the confrontation with Japan, which could have raised concerns about whether the administration had done enough to prevent it. After several days of deliberation, Woodrow Wilson gave a long and controversial statement of about 3,700 words on 2 April 1917, securing a declaration of war against Germany from a divided Congress. FDR's message was only 503 words long and seven minutes long, making it the shortest significant policy address delivered by a president on record. It requested that the joint session of Congress proclaim a state of war between the United States and Japan. The legislators needed only thirty-three minutes to pass a nearly unanimous resolution (one Representative opposed), which Roosevelt signed a few hours later at the White House.

Despite Pearl Harbor, FDR insisted that Germany remained America's principal adversary. Hitler's declaration of war on the United States on December 11, 1941, preempted the need to discover a casus belli, which Roosevelt would not have shied away from. Since Munich showed the unquenchable extent of its leader's goals, he had seen Nazi Germany's destruction as critical to America. Hitler's aggression, according to FDR, constituted an existential threat to the American way of life, which was predicated on the survival of a liberal and civilized international civilization. In his yearly presentation to Congress in 1939, he predicted US war goals by proclaiming,

There comes a time in men's affairs when they must be prepared to defend not just their homes, but also the tenets of faith and humanity upon which their churches, governments, and civilizations are built. The fight for religion, democracy, and good faith across nations is all the same. To save one, we must collectively decide to save all.

When the United States entered World War II, Roosevelt transitioned from diplomat-in-chief to commander-in-chief, pursuing triumph against foes who attacked American ideals and national-security president seeking a peace that upheld them.

8

Commander-in-chief

Structures and strategies

Franklin D. Roosevelt embraced his duty as commander-in-chief of the armed forces more than any other president in American history. 'Every president has possessed the Constitutional authority which that title implies, but few presidents have shared Mr Roosevelt's preparedness to apply it in practice, in detail, and with such resolve,' writes Mark Watson, an official Army historian of World War II. Commander-in-chief became his favored title during the war, as evidenced by his directive to Secretary of State Cordell Hull to address him as such rather than as 'Mr President' while proposing a toast at a Cabinet luncheon in January 1942. Except for the Civil War, the Second World War was the most serious crisis in American history. FDR faced the responsibilities of leadership in war with calm assurance, as he had done throughout the Great Depression, which had now been relegated to third place in the republic's panoply of threats. When the difficult first year of US involvement in the conflict came to an end, his confidential secretary, William Hassett, observed that he remained 'unruffled in temper, buoyant of spirit... and can sleep anywhere whenever opportunity affords - priceless assets for one bearing his burdens, which he never mentions'.

FDR was a more engaged, inventive, and capable commander-in-chief than British Prime Minister Winston Churchill or Soviet dictator Joseph Stalin in military matters. He was the only Allied commander with a truly global vision, and he was deeply involved in keeping the US-UK-USSR Grand Alliance together and devising its plan to fight the Axis forces. The institutional arrangements he built during the war to coordinate US military and foreign affairs lay the groundwork for the National Security Act of 1947, which codified policy-making organizations to wage the Cold War. On the home front, FDR rallied the nation in the face of early military setbacks, educated the people about the importance of a Germany-first strategy before pivoting to defeat Japan, and directed the economic miracle in which American industry frequently exceeded military production targets that had previously been thought unattainable. His wartime leadership was also essential in expanding presidential power, sometimes to the point of exceeding constitutional authority. Later historians would consider this as the beginning of the 'imperial presidency,' but Roosevelt did not claim inherent presidential right to act as he did, as some successors did.

The first problem FDR faced was establishing a command structure that would support his decision to be the sole coordinator of US military strategy and foreign policy during the war. In September 1939, the Joint Army-Navy Board (JANB) was moved into the Executive Office of the President (EOP), ensuring that the service chiefs reported directly to him rather than the Secretaries of War and Navy. When America entered the war, Roosevelt followed the informal approach he had devised with military advisers in 1940-1. He regarded lines of duty as something to be followed when they served his objectives and avoided when they did not. As a result, he created a bespoke commander-in-chief structure that allowed him to get what he wanted from his most valuable subordinates. He reserved the power to overrule the service chiefs on all strategic decisions, sometimes on military grounds and sometimes on political reasons, especially when it came to alliance affairs, after consulting with them on all strategic topics. Roosevelt, never intimidated by military status, overruled the service chiefs on strategic considerations at least twenty-two times between late 1938 and the end of 1944, according to the Army chief historian's count.

The service chiefs, accustomed to transparent chains of command and hierarchical patterns of operation, were never happy with Roosevelt's leadership style but adapted to it. Army Chief of Staff George Marshall insisted on preserving a formal connection with the president, refusing invites to Hyde Park, ignoring requests to drop by the White House for a late-afternoon martini, and refusing to be addressed by his first name. When asked for his opinion, Marshall provided it in an honest and brief manner. He advised his service commanders to make their written reports to FDR brief and to the point. 'Papers, lengthy talks, and anything short of a few pungent phrases of description rapidly bore the president,' he recommended. Marshall's decision on this point is called into doubt by FDR's practice of directing regular written queries at his military chiefs in order to keep them on their toes.

Roosevelt intervened less in Army matters and more in Navy matters, where he claimed better competence. Marshall had no trouble convincing him to approve plans for the Army's most dramatic organizational changes since the early twentieth century, which included limiting direct access to the chief of staff to six officers (down from sixty-one previously), creating three'super commands' (Army Ground Forces, Army Air Forces, and Services and Supply), and replacing the old General Headquarters and War Plans Division with a new Operations Division to plan gl

FDR opposed a comparable consolidation of control for the Navy in order to maintain his influence over assignments and promotions, force deployment, and even vessel construction. Despite the fact that the United States was short on P-C submarine chasers, which were considered critical for convoy protection, Roosevelt insisted on transferring two of them to Brazil to protect its commerce fleet after it declared war on Germany in August 1942. 'This is an issue of international relations that must be carried out regardless of simply military desirability,' he told skeptical Navy chiefs. Furthermore, his admirals did not share his desire for heavy cruisers and light aircraft carriers. The Navy command was shocked when he authorized through backchannels industry billionaire Henry Kaiser's concept for prefabricated light carrier construction, which it had already rejected.

Meanwhile, FDR maneuvered deftly to maintain control over the new organizational structures set up to coordinate Anglo-American war planning. From 22 December 1941 to 14 January 1942, US and

British military commanders met in Washington to prepare strategy for the European and Pacific theaters in conjunction with Roosevelt and Churchill. The talks resulted in an agreement to form an Anglo-American Combined Chiefs of Staff (CCS) with the authority to do strategic planning for both countries while reporting only to the president and prime minister for ultimate approval. To achieve parity with the UK Chiefs of Staff Committee, members of which served on the CCS, Roosevelt renamed the JANB the US Joint Chiefs of Staff (JCS). He also asked that the new group oversee the entire war strategy from Washington.

Churchill had preferred separate committees in London and Washington to be in charge of European and Pacific strategy, but agreed to a single command headquarters in Washington in acknowledgment that the United States would eventually contribute the majority of people and materials. FDR persuaded the prime minister, on Marshall's advice, to agree to the appointment of supreme commanders to direct air, ground, and naval operations in each theater of the war, a proposal opposed by his own Navy chiefs (who disliked the idea of any Army man in command of their ships) and the British. To appease Churchill, FDR agreed to appoint one of his generals, Sir Archibald Wavell, to oversee ABDACOM (American-British-Dutch-Australian Command) in the South Pacific, a role that was shortly abolished due to Japanese advances. In addition, he decided that Field Marshal Sir John Dill would act as the prime minister's personal representative on the CCS and would be based in Washington on a permanent basis to liaise with the JCS. Churchill also wanted the Munitions Assignment Board, the most important of the Arcadia sub-boards (the others being Shipping Adjustment, Raw Materials, Production, and Resources), separated into two divisions that could work independently of the CCS in Washington and London. Roosevelt saw this as a ruse to give Britain control over American military production and refused to participate.

The eventual outcome of this high-level maneuvering was that Roosevelt retained strategic authority at his fingertips. Churchill embraced the new procedures as a way of securing FDR's commitment to the joint war effort, certain that his apparently superior knowledge and greater experience in military affairs would ensure his dominance over Anglo-American combined strategy. Lord Moran, his physician, had a deeper understanding of what he had conceded, writing in his journal, 'The Americans have had their way, and the war will be run from Washington.' Sir Alan Brooke, the new Army Chief of Staff, thought the Arcadia organizational arrangement was "wild and half-baked" in giving the Americans key leadership of the war when their forces were "totally unprepared to play a major role," but resentfully acknowledged it was a "fait accompli."

FDR regarded the new JCS with the same casualness that he did the JANB. Dill, who was used to the hierarchical British system, exclaimed, 'The whole organization belongs to the days of George Washington.' The service chiefs wanted more structure, therefore they demanded regular meetings with written minutes documenting debates and conclusions. Instead, Roosevelt continued to see them as a group or individually whenever he pleased, and he banned written records from being kept during their early contacts. 'Put that thing up,' he told Major General John Deane, the JCS secretary who had brought a large notepad to the organization's inaugural White House meeting. However, by late 1942, FDR understood the value of minute discussions in order to keep track of where the JCS stood on second-front problems.

Another cause of military angst was the lack of a clear charter outlining JCS powers. FDR eventually signed a declaration produced by the British and American service commanders that provided a broad outline of CCS authority, but no record exists of Churchill ever co-approving it. In contrast, the president declined to bind his hands by formally granting JCS powers. 'It would bring no benefits and might limit operational flexibility in some way,' he told the leaders. As a result, the JCS existed solely at his discretion, with no official status established by statute or executive order. As its chairman later stated, 'I have heard that in some file there is a chit or memorandum from Roosevelt setting up the Joint Chiefs, but I never saw it.' FDR ensured that the JCS remained a useful, malleable, and dedicated instrument of his will as commander-in-chief in this manner.

Membership in the JCS was not set in stone. The group consisted of George Marshall, Army Air Force chief Lieutenant General Henry 'Hap' Arnold, Chief of Naval Operations (CNO) Admiral Harold Stark, and Commander-in-Chief of the US Fleet Admiral Ernest King when it began holding regular Tuesday meetings in the Public Health Building on Nineteenth Street. Despite not being a service leader, Arnold attended because Marshall was a strong supporter of strategic air power and needed two Army votes to counterbalance Navy involvement. 'I attempted to give Arnold as much power as I could,' his supervisor eventually admitted. 'I attempted to make him as close to the Chief of Staff of the Air Force as I could.' Stark departed his desk job in Washington in March 1942 to head US naval forces in Europe, putting him out of reach of congressional probes over the Navy's lack of preparation for the Pearl Harbor attack. The president immediately signed an executive order broadening King's powers to include CNO. As a result, the Navy now equaled the Army in having a single chief of staff responsible for both staff and fighting forces. It also produced an imbalance in the JCS, which Marshall attempted to correct by convincing FDR to nominate a senior Navy officer as chairman. Admiral William Leahy, a former CNO and current Ambassador to Vichy France, was the man Hitler had in mind.

Following his recall from Vichy, the president finally appointed Leahy to chair the JCS in July 1942, after much prodding from Marshall. The assignment effectively ended efforts from Republicans (including Wendell Willkie), some Democrats, and a sizable number of newspapers for the appointment of General Douglas MacArthur as commander of a united Army-Navy-Air command to lead the war. Roosevelt, aware that MacArthur was not the military genius his supporters assumed, never gave this thought. Marshall believed that Leahy would improve the flow of information between the White House and the JCS, making it the pivot of an organized strategic decision-making process. FDR's opposing goal was reflected in

Leahy's position as 'Chief of Staff to the Commander-in-Chief,' whose function it was to represent his views and interests on the JCS. When asked if Leahy would be subject to Senate confirmation in his new position, Trump stated that his commander-in-chief's right to issue any serving officer "an order of duty" rendered this unnecessary. During a lengthy interview before the appointment, the admiral conveyed his knowledge of the job. 'The Joint Chiefs of Staff was an instrument of the Commander-in-Chief and was accountable to him,' Leahy said afterwards. I represented him on the committee.' As a seasoned diplomat, he served as an effective chair in resolving inter-service disagreements within the JCS, keeping the president's concerns in the forefront and working as a conduit to ensure that FDR had the information he needed to make choices as war leader.

Leahy, who was given an office in the freshly reconstructed East Wing of the White House, met with FDR on a daily basis during his first eighteen months in office. He subsequently said, "Churchill and Roosevelt really ran the war." 'We [the British and American chiefs] were essentially artisans, constructing patterns of strategy from the basic blueprints entrusted to us by our respective Commanders-in-Chief,' said one. In truth, FDR's direct engagement in military affairs dwindled as the war continued, partly due to plans he had overseen genesis moving into action and partly due to his physical infirmities in 1944-5. As his trust in his chiefs developed, he reduced his control of their operational actions while never giving them complete authority. As a result, US strategy remained remarkably consistent throughout the war, embodying Roosevelt's insistence on maintaining support for Britain, Russia, and China, the imperative of crushing Germany before Japan and demanding unconditional surrender of both, and the need for a postwar 'United Nations' organization supported and directed by the Big Four powers. According to historian Eric Larrabee, 'it was a comprehensive program, in which war and politics were integrated to a degree rarely seen, and he persevered with it from start to finish.'

FDR's leadership style meant that he never built a command center like Churchill's war rooms in Whitehall, but after viewing the portable one the prime minister took to Arcadia, he had a map room constructed in the White House. What he desired was a secure area to keep maps that would allow him to track the progress of the war and secret cables, notably from Allied commanders. The map room was built in a ground-floor cloakroom measuring only 24 feet by 19 feet in March 1942. It served as FDR's private reference center, but he made the majority of his crucial judgments in the Oval Office and the Oval Room private study adjoining his bedroom in the White House living quarters. He used these facilities to consult the JCS and deal with Allied communications. Incoming messages were received and decrypted using Army channels, while outgoing messages were enciphered and dispatched through Navy lines, thus Roosevelt had a complete set of both.

America experienced early setbacks in the Pacific War, for which military strategy was still in its infancy. The Japanese pursued a multi-pronged strategy aimed at gaining control of the Dutch East Indies to replenish petroleum reserves, establishing an unbreakable hold over Southeast Asia, and forcing China into submission by cutting off its external supply routes. Once achieved, the Imperial Government thought that the United States would be intimidated into petitioning for peace in acknowledgement of its unrivaled power in the Pacific. To be successful in this venture, Japan had to first protect the eastern flank of its 'Southern Operation' by launching a surprise attack on the US Pacific fleet based at Pearl Harbor, then destroy the massive British naval facility at Singapore, and finally seize control of the Philippines to prevent the US from using it as a forward base to disrupt naval operations and troop movements.

The attack on Pearl Harbor was carried out by 350 aircraft launched from six carriers that had gone to a location 200 miles north of Hawaii. It sank or severely damaged 18 ships, including eight battleships, destroyed nearly 180 planes and severely damaged another 120, and killed 2,403 troops. The United States had never before suffered such large-scale naval losses in a single combat. The three aircraft carriers typically stationed at Pearl Harbor escaped the carnage while on maneuvers, but the strike put the Pacific fleet in severe difficulties. Because of the Magic intelligence breakthrough, American codebreakers were able to follow high-level diplomatic dispatches from Tokyo to the Japanese Embassy in Washington, which offered advance warning of an attack but not its location. Because US naval intelligence felt that Japanese airplanes had the fuel capacity to launch an attack from so far out at sea that they would not be noticed, Pearl Harbor appeared to be the least likely target, but technological advances had enlarged their flight radius. The Japanese were completely caught off guard when they launched a pinpoint hit on a target 4,000 miles distant from their homeland and only 2,000 miles from the US mainland.

This was the first move in a concerted offensive spanning the North Pacific to the Indian Ocean. On 10 December 1941, two British battleships, the Prince of Wales and the Repulse, were sunk off the coast of Malaya by carrier-launched aircraft; Hong Kong, Guam, and Wake Island were attacked; and lightning invasions launched from Indo-China proceeded through Malaysia and Thailand into Burma by mid-January 1942. Meanwhile, Japanese forces advanced rapidly down the Malay peninsula towards the ostensibly impregnable Singapore, whose 85,000-strong garrison surrendered on 15 February 1942, marking the British military's worst defeat in history. The devastating defeat of the hastily prepared ABDACOM navy in the Battle of the Java Sea on 27 February allowed the Dutch East Indies to be captured on 12 March.

The day after Pearl Harbor, another Japanese air raid obliterated American air strength in the Philippines, leaving this US colony vulnerable to invasion on December 22. According to War Department plans, 80,000 American and Filipino combat forces led by General Douglas MacArthur retreated from Manila to the Bataan peninsula and the neighboring island fortress of Corregidor (joined by 25,000 civilian evacuees). Starvation and sickness gradually eroded their ability to maintain these defensive positions. In order to declare itself neutral, disband its army, and demand that all foreign forces leave its land, President Manuel Quezon approached the

American government in early February 1942 for immediate independence (legally due in 1946).

Military planners in the United States had long recognized that the Philippines could not be held against a Japanese onslaught. Nonetheless, Roosevelt rejected Quezon's plan, fearing that neutralization would signify America's inability to bear enormous losses. While accepting local soldiers' surrender, he swore, 'As long as the flag of the United States flies on Filipino territory as a pledge of our loyalty to your people, it will be defended to the death.' '[W]e cannot exhibit weakness in spirit, no matter how physically weak we may currently be in any particular theater,' MacArthur, who advocated neutrality, said. It is imperative that complete evidence be established once and for all in the minds of all peoples that the American determination and indomitable will to victory continues down to the last unit.' As a result, US resistance in the Philippines had to last "as long as humanly possible."

These letters had the desired effect of hardening the resolve of their recipients. Despite FDR's plans to evacuate Quezon and his entourage on February 20, Filipino forces fought with their American counterparts to the terrible end. Roosevelt rescinded his no-surrender decree on April 8, recognizing that further sacrifice was fruitless. The famished and ill Bataan contingent surrendered the next day, and the men on Corregidor did the same on May 6. Despite its failure, the Philippines campaign increased FDR's moral authority as commander-in-chief. George Marshall had evolved from a kind peacetime politician to a steely war leader willing to lose soldiers in battle. When FDR rejected Filipino neutralization, he said, "I immediately discarded everything in my mind I had held to his discredit." I decided he was a wonderful dude.'

Roosevelt also showed his ability as commander-in-chief in dealing with the most visible and self-serving of America's wartime theater commanders. When MacArthur was brought out of retirement to lead US Army forces in the Far East in mid-1941, he botched his defense of the Philippines. When Japanese planes attacked Manila's Clark Field on December 8, he allowed a fleet of eighteen Flying Fortress bombers and fifty-three fighter planes to be caught on the ground. He then failed to move food and medical supplies from well-stocked storage depots to keep Bataan and Corregidor defended. A lesser besieging army of Japanese simply waited for famine and sickness to force their opponents to surrender. Never one to accept failure, MacArthur meticulously depicted himself as a military mastermind via daily press releases, many of which he wrote himself, from his underground headquarters in the Malinta Tunnel on Corregidor. Meanwhile, he appealed with FDR for an offensive naval plan to assault the enemy's scattered armies in East Asia's marine supply lanes. 'The only way to beat him is to battle him relentlessly,' he asserted. From my current vantage position, I may be able to view the entire Pacific strategy more clearly than anyone else.'

Roosevelt would have been justified in dismissing the errant general, but he chose not to do so - and not simply because of his political connections. Knowing that taking MacArthur prisoner would provide the Japanese with a great propaganda coup, FDR authorized his transfer to command of Allied forces in the Southwest Pacific. On the night of March 12, the general, his wife and four-year-old son, as well as seventeen members of his staff, were evacuated from Corregidor on four PT boats that circumnavigated the Japanese blockade to reach safety on the island of Mindanao, from which they were flown to Australia. When he arrived, MacArthur informed reporters that his duty was to "organize the American offensive against Japan, the primary goal of which is the relief of the Philippines." I passed through and will return.' This assertion of strategic power was not met with a presidential censure. Following meetings with FDR in late January, Harry Hopkins wrote in his diary that some high-ranking Army and Navy officers were afraid to take "great and bold risks," and that they would "have to be liquidated before we really get on with our fighting." Regardless of his flaws, MacArthur wanted to take the battle to the enemy, which made him vital to Roosevelt as a symbol of America's unwavering pursuit of triumph. FDR possessed the self-assurance not to resent the adoration he earned from a press and public yearning for heroes, as well as the personal authority to keep him in line.

Of all, FDR was the primary source of motivation for most Americans during the war. Sensing a need to lift spirits amid news of military setbacks, he scheduled a Fireside Chat on 23 February 1942 that relied on listeners referring to their own maps while he explained the importance of strange places that many of them have never heard of - places that are now the battlefield for civilization'. On the day of the speech, numerous newspapers placed maps of the world on their front pages at the president's request. FDR told speechwriter Samuel Rosenman, "I'd like to explain to the people something about geography - what our problem is and what the overall strategy of this war must be." I want to explain it to them in ABC terms so that they understand what is going on and how each battle fits into the picture... if they grasp the problem and what we are driving for, I am confident that they can take any kind of bad news on the chin.

Speaking the day following Washington's birthday, Roosevelt reminded an estimated 61.3 million people that the Continental Army had shown great moral tenacity to win the War of Independence despite early losses, and he expressed confidence that America would similarly triumph over its modern-day foes. 'This battle,' he proclaimed, 'is a new sort of war. It is warfare in terms of every continent, every island, and every airplane in the world.' 'Look at your map,' he said again and again, explaining the significance of 'the world-encircling battle lines' that necessitated America to fight at distances that extended all the way around the globe. The far-flung theaters of war were all geo-strategically interwoven in the United Nations' drive, cited eleven times in the address, to establish a victorious peace based on aggressor disarmament, nation self-determination, and safeguards of basic human rights. As a result, according to one historian, 'his global thinking, on a geographical plane, reemerged as universal thinking on an ideological plane.'

In complete contrast to the paean to individual liberties in the Fireside Chat, Roosevelt had just four days earlier ordered the most brazen mass violation of American individuals' freedoms ever perpetrated by the federal government. Executive Order 9066 enabled the Secretary of War to 'prescribe military regions... from which any or all individuals may be barred' by imposing whatever limitations were considered necessary, as well as to arrange for the transportation, food, and housing of evacuees. The edict, which was written in such a way that it might apply everywhere in the United States, was directed only at Japanese-American inhabitants of California, Oregon, and Washington. It led to the expulsion and subsequent incarceration of 120,000 persons, 70% of whom were born in the United States. Initially housed in substandard temporary facilities, Japanese Americans were detained by the end of 1942 in purpose-built facilities, effectively concentration camps ringed with towers, gates, and barbed wire ranging from eastern California to south-eastern Arkansas. Roosevelt established the War Relocation Authority inside the EOP to manage these facilities, but he was cautious to separate himself from its shameful goal. In February 1944, he transferred the agency to the Department of the Interior, an unusual limitation of his executive authority.

FDR never explained why he sanctioned the most heinous episode of his presidency. There was no evidence of Japanese-American treason, despite rumors of fifth-column operations to promote invasion or sabotage. This didn't stop General John DeWitt, commander of the Army's Western Defense Command, from proclaiming, 'A Jap's a Jap. It doesn't matter whether he's an American citizen or not. I don't want any of them.' In public or private, Roosevelt said nothing to imply that he shared such apparent prejudice. In response to congressional charges that the internees were living too well off Uncle Sam, he declared in September 1943, 'In vindication of the very ideals for which we are fighting this war, it is important to us to maintain a high standard of fair, equal, and considerate treatment for people of this minority as well as people of all other minorities.'

FDR's support for internment was almost certainly motivated by political considerations. He was well aware that Woodrow Wilson's loss of congressional control in the 1918 midterm elections had jeopardized his peace-treaty aspirations. Keeping Democratic supporters in Pacific-coast states on board by catering to their anti-Japanese views was a method to prevent the same outcome as the 1942 midterm elections. When Americans learned about Imperial Army crimes against prisoners of war, particularly the Bataan death march that followed the Philippines' capitulation, their rage grew to national proportions. As a result, before running for a fourth term, FDR refused to allow the internees to return to their West Coast homes, a restoration that was acceptable to the War Department by mid-1944 because the security threat had passed. Roosevelt's handling of Japanese Americans during WWII, according to author Roger Daniels, "is a permanent deserved stain on his reputation."

Executive Order 9066 was a gross misuse of authority in depriving American individuals of their rights on flimsy security grounds, but it was not a solo presidential initiative. By making refusal to leave a certain area when commanded a federal felony, Congress effectively endorsed FDR's directive. In June 1943, the Supreme Court ruled unanimously in two cases to sustain coercive incarceration based on military necessity. This agreement was only broken when the war came to a close in the Korematsu case, which resulted in a split decision in which one of three dissenting justices, Frank Murphy, criticized Japanese-American incarceration as "legalization of racism."

FDR's wartime approach to presidential authority was exemplified by the internment policy. He had mostly established the New Deal through legislative means, but beginning in early 1941, he began to use commander-in-chief prerogatives to stake out policy fait accomplis that Congress confirmed in statutes such as the War Powers Acts of December 1941 and March 1942. The realities of war compelled him to depend more heavily on his proclamation of 'unlimited national emergency' in May 1941, which gave him authority as commander-in-chief to take steps necessary to protect the nation. The public's backing for the president's broad use of emergency powers compelled Congress and the courts to follow suit.

Roosevelt's broad interpretation of his commander-in-chief mandate enabled him to consolidate roughly fifty new war-management organizations under the all-purpose Office of Emergency Management. With the exception of the Office of Price Administration, which was specifically designated by statute as the agency with the largest impact on people's lives and hence the most in need of public approval, Congress merely accepted the others on the assumption that the president ordered their necessity. FDR's assumption of unilateral authority peaked on September 7, 1942, when he declared that he would refuse to sign the Emergency Price Control Act unless Congress eliminated an inflationary farm parity provision. 'The President has the powers, under the Constitution and Congressional statutes, to take actions necessary to avert a tragedy that would interfere with the victory of the war,' he declared. Nonetheless, he was keen to highlight that if peace was restored, 'the powers under which I act immediately revert to the people - to whom they belong'. As Arthur Schlesinger put it, Roosevelt "knew where he wanted to go and where he thought the country had to go." But he didn't want to travel there by himself.'

To win the war, the United States had to get more involved in fighting it. Six months after the attack on Pearl Harbor, the United States had not conquered an inch of enemy territory, had not defeated the Japanese in a significant battle, and had not launched an offensive campaign, but that was about to change. A daring operation of relatively minor military significance, done at FDR's request, was indirectly responsible for Japan's first loss of the war. In retribution for the attack on Pearl Harbor, Roosevelt planned an air strike on Tokyo to disturb the Japanese idea of invincibility and display America's tenacity. In response, the JCS authorized the launch of sixteen Army B-25 bombers from the Navy carrier Hornet as part of a small task force that proceeded into the Pacific to within 600 miles of Tokyo. Lieutenant Colonel James Doolittle assembled and trained a volunteer squad of highly skilled aviators for the mission he oversaw. Roosevelt realized the risk of high-value airmen being killed during a pilot shortage, but thought it was worth it to shake enemy confidence.

The raid, which took place on April 18, 1942, caused minimal physical damage, but all of the planes arrived in Tokyo and returned as planned to the coastal region of eastern China, where the crews either crashed-landed or bailed out. Although eight airmen were captured by the Japanese, the others received prompt assistance from local Chinese to reach safe havens. These citizens paid a horrific price in the form of wholesale killings, mass rapes, and widespread destruction carried out by Imperial troops deployed to seize the area where the American planes crashed. Roosevelt had not given the Chinese government advance warning of the operation because he expected a reaction but not on such a large scale.

The human repercussions of the Doolittle raid were unimaginably awful, but the military consequences were crucial to the war. It dealt a psychological blow to Japan's military chiefs, who had failed in their terrified responsibility to safeguard the Emperor and the Homeland. Admiral Isoroku Yamamoto, the mastermind of the Pearl Harbor attack, felt this the most. A subordinate later remembered, 'In [his] mind, the concept that Tokyo, the Emperor's seat, must be kept safe from an air strike amounted to an obsession.' Yamamoto persuaded the Navy General Staff to postpone preparations for amphibious invasions of a string of Melanesian islands stretching from New Guinea to Samoa in order to cut Australia's naval links with America. Instead, he obtained approval for an effort to destroy the US Pacific fleet, removing the threat of carrier-launched air strikes on Japan. To entice it away from Pearl Harbor for a decisive fight, he intended to strike Midway Island, an American-held atoll 1,100 miles to the south-east, believed critical for Hawaii's defense.

The Battle of Midway, which took place from June 4 to 7, ultimately ended Japanese naval dominance in the Pacific. FDR chose Admiral Chester Nimitz over a number of senior officers to head the Pacific fleet ten days after the attack on Pearl Harbor. 'The one important thing about him,' said Admiral Raymond Spruance, battle commander at Midway, 'was that he was always ready to fight... And he wanted officers who would press the war with the Japanese. If they refused, they were transferred elsewhere.' Because the Pacific theater was too large for Nimitz to be a seagoing commander, he placed a high value on selecting the right subordinates. Rather than sailing with the fleet, he stayed in Pearl Harbor to deal with organization, planning, and communication. In recognition of his abilities, FDR promoted him to supreme commander of Allied forces in the north, central, and south-eastern Pacific in February 1942, a position George Marshall desired for Douglas MacArthur.

Nimitz bet on the Japanese navy hitting Midway rather than other probable targets, guided by his own Magic code-breakers. Despite sending a diversionary force north to the Aleutians, Yamamoto commanded a large armada of eight carriers and nearly 700 aircraft to take on an American force of three carriers, eight cruisers, and fifteen destroyers. Despite being close in the early phases, the fight culminated in a Trafalgar-scale defeat for the Imperial Navy. Staggering Japanese casualties, primarily as a result of aerial battle, included four carriers sunk by the US, a loss of 1,332 planes destroyed to 147 for the US, and approximately 3,000 killed (including many of their best pilots) to 307 Americans. Nimitz wasted no time in rubbing salt in the wounds of his adversaries. In declaring victory, he stated that "Pearl Harbor has now been partially avenged." 'Vengeance will not be complete until Japanese maritime might is rendered ineffective... we are about halfway there.'

The US invasion of Guadalcanal, a 2,500-square-mile island, two months later marked the first stage towards recapturing the Solomons. In May, the Japanese took neighboring Tulagi with its deep-water anchorage as part of their campaign to seize the Melanesian islands that encircle Australia. The Guadalcanal offensive, conceived by Ernest King as a Navy and Marine operation, got Roosevelt's approval because it promised action in the shape of the first US amphibious landings since the Spanish-

American War of 1898. When it became clear that more resources would be required, the JCS authorized the contribution of Army forces, both ground and aviation, a decision made more urgent by the knowledge that the Japanese were constructing an airstrip on Guadalcanal.

The Marine landings on August 7 were originally successful, but the Imperial Navy's stunning victory at Savo Island on the night of August 8-9 forced the US Pacific fleet to temporarily evacuate, allowing the enemy to rush in significant troop reinforcements. By mid-October, Nimitz had determined that the American situation was "not hopeless, but...certainly critical." Roosevelt directed the JCS to "ensure that every possible weapon gets into that area to hold Guadalcanal, and that having held it in this crisis, munitions and planes and crews are on their way to take advantage of our success." Significant reinforcements and resupplies arrived quickly, but transport vessels remained scarce until William Leahy, acting on presidential authority, directed the War Shipping Administration to 'provide without delay twenty additional ships... for use in the South Pacific'.

FDR felt more directly involved in the battle for Guadalcanal than in any other campaign. He cited it in six press briefings between August 1942 and November 1943, more than any other wartime incident. Fighting on land, sea, and air to hold a small atoll primarily covered by clammy, fetid, and malarial jungle was among the Pacific war's most fierce. The longer it went on, the more vital the outcome became for both sides, prompting them to commit significantly more resources to victory than they had planned. The Japanese were forced to evacuate in February 1943 due to unsustainable losses. Despite the fact that both sides lost roughly the same number of ships, the Imperial Navy was substantially weaker because the US could replenish its losses with greater ease. The destruction of nearly 800 Japanese planes and pilots dealt the enemy an even larger blow. Finally, the Imperial Army's self-image as invincible jungle fighters was shattered by the score of 24,000 personnel killed or taken prisoner against US losses of less than 1,600. The Solomons became a battleground for the rest of the war, where the US could wear down Japan's more restricted military resources. In June 1943, after learning of another naval victory, FDR told William Hassett, 'Our battle of attrition is doing its thing.'

As the marines prepared to land on Guadalcanal, FDR was arguing with his top military advisers on where to launch the United States' first ground offensive against Hitler. Initially, the president endorsed an Army proposal for a second front in Western Europe to divert German forces away from the Russian invasion. General Dwight D. Eisenhower, the Army's chief planner, devised three operations code-named Bolero, Sledgehammer, and Roundup, which were approved after thorough consideration by George Marshall and endorsed by the other chiefs. Sledgehammer was an emergency small-scale invasion in 1942 to establish a foothold in Cherbourg that would draw German divisions away from the eastern front if the Red Army appeared to be in danger of collapsing, and Roundup envisaged a full-scale invasion of France in the spring of 1943.

According to Roosevelt, 'it was important to draw off pressure on the Russians who... are presently killing off more Germans and destroying more equipment than you and I put together,' as he wrote to Churchill. While the British saw Sledgehammer as a suicide mission and a 1943 invasion as premature, they kept their misgivings to themselves in case the Americans opted for a Pacific-first policy if European operations were postponed. Fortunately for them, FDR quickly changed his mind about the Army plan since it would not ensure what he sorely desired, a second front in 1942. After receiving intelligence from Ambassador William Leahy that French forces in Morocco and Algeria were so disillusioned with the Vichy regime that they would not resist an Anglo-American invasion of North Africa, an operation Churchill had previously proposed in vain under the code name Gymnast, an alternative took shape in his mind. On April 18, FDR directed Harry Hopkins, who was in London at the time to press the case for Bolero-Sledgehammer-Roundup, to notify Churchill that Gymnast might be back in play. An 'eyes-only' presidential communication to his military leaders in early May stated categorically that 'there was a need for very high speed in developing actual operations' in the Atlantic theater 'in 1942 - not 1943'.

Once the Japanese naval threat to India was removed by Midway, Churchill felt empowered to express his own objections to Sledgehammer - and to do it face to face with the president. When he arrived in Washington on June 19, he went immediately to Hyde Park for meetings with Roosevelt and Hopkins. There, he presented a memorandum explaining why the operation could not succeed: the Allies lacked trained troops and landing craft at the time, the Wehrmacht divisions in France were sufficient to deal with a small invasion without reinforcements from the eastern front, and French civilians would face massive retaliation for assisting the invaders. If an early cross-channel assault was unfeasible, Churchill realized that the Allies must not stand inactive in the Atlantic theater' for the rest of 1942. As a result, he suggested Gymnast as a project that would "fit within the general structure of BOLERO" and "take some of the weight off Russia."

By this time, FDR's service commanders, with the support of Secretary of War Henry Stimson, had communicated their belief that the quickest way to win in Europe was to assemble overwhelming forces in Britain in 1942, invade northern France in 1943, and then drive into Germany. Gymnast, they believe, would push back the timeline by diverting resources from Bolero, would be vulnerable to German air and armored counter-attacks, and would deplete naval resources presently committed in the North Atlantic to secure supply routes to Britain and Russia. To address the matter, Roosevelt and Churchill proceeded to Washington on 21 June for additional talks, which were interrupted by news of the capitulation of the 33,000-strong garrison of Tobruk, reputedly the unbreakable British stronghold in Libya, to Erwin Rommel's Afrika Korps. In a show of solidarity, FDR decided to divert 300 new Sherman tanks destined for US armored divisions to assist the British Eighth Army in defending Egypt and the Suez Canal from the invading Germans, a transfer that Marshall completed by the end of the day with the addition of 100 howitzers. It was preferable in these circumstances to avoid a controversial resolution of the second-front issue. What resulted was a shambles: shared commitment to Bolero, continuous evaluation of Sledgehammer's feasibility, and examination of alternatives, including Gymnast.

Knowing that FDR was determined to have American troops fighting in the Atlantic theater in 1942, Churchill cabled on his way back to London that Gymnast alone could meet this requirement. An enraged Marshall interpreted this as a British ruse to postpone the assault of France in 1943 by diverting resources into a North African diversion. He obtained support for a Pacific-first strategy at the JCS meeting on 10 July if Churchill did not back down on Gymnast, a course suggested to FDR in a memorandum signed together with King. Marshall emphasized in a supplementary communication to the president that, in the absence of Britain's unwavering commitment to Bolero-Roundup, the US should go all-out to defeat Japan while maintaining a defensive posture with token forces in the European theater.

FDR had no intention of relinquishing his commander-in-chief authority over war policy. Furthermore, he saw no sense in changing the focus to the Pacific and allowing Hitler free rein in Europe for the two years or so it would take to overcome Japan. After reviewing the Marshall-King memorandum in Hyde Park on Sunday, July 12, he phoned the War Department and demanded a comprehensive plan for a major Pacific offensive, an explanation of how it would help the Soviet Union, and an assessment of its benefits for the global situation by the end of the day. By any standard, what was achieved in a few hours of frenetic work was completely inadequate. The presidential response was a sharp rap on the military knuckles:

I carefully read your Sunday forecast. My first reaction is that it is exactly what Germany hoped the US would do after the attack on Pearl Harbor. Second, it does not authorize the use of American troops in combat save on a small number of islands whose possession will have no impact on the global situation this year or next. Third, it is neither beneficial to Russia or the Middle East.

As a result, it is now disapproved. He then had an assistant read a five-page telephone message to Marshall and King, stating that US forces would have to fight in the Atlantic theater in 1942, either through Sledgehammer or another operation if Sledgehammer was not feasible. 'Gymnast might not be decisive, but it would weaken Germany, rescue the Middle East, and make Italy susceptible to our air force,' it concluded. The war will be won in Europe and Africa this year, not in the Pacific. 'I believe we're doing well in the Pacific.'

On his return to the White House, Roosevelt exchanged strong words with Marshall about the second front. Years later, the general explained FDR's stance as a result of "political necessity." He claimed that the military had failed to recognize that "the leader in a democracy must keep the people entertained... People demand action." Roosevelt probably planned military operations in North Africa to begin before the 1942 midterm elections, ideally on October 30. Refusing to put politics ahead of caution, he agreed to Marshall's plea for a seven-day postponement to ensure that assault forces were sufficiently prepared and supplied. Sledgehammer, on the other hand, would almost certainly have been a sacrifice operation, with high losses lost for no tangible return. As commander-in-chief, Roosevelt chose a less risky operation with a better probability of success and the potential to contribute more to Germany's final defeat. The lack of war experience of American forces, as well as the Allies' lack of control of the North Atlantic (gained in the second half of 1943), made this the correct military option, but it delayed the cross-channel invasion of France until June 1944.

To win consent for a coordinated operation in 1942, FDR dispatched Marshall and King, accompanied by Hopkins, to London with instructions signed 'Commander-in-Chief'. Knowing that Sledgehammer would be rejected outright by the British, he paved the way for Gymnast by directing the trio that the 'cardinal principles' to guide the selection of where to strike would be speed of decision on plans, unity of plans, and assault mixed with defense but not defense alone'. North Africa was the only location that satisfied these requirements. Roosevelt gave Marshall and King one week from their arrival in London on July 19 to resolve the issue; Sledgehammer died within three days, killed by the British War Cabinet's outright rejection of it; and the US chiefs accepted Gymnast, renamed Torch, the very next day. Churchill agreed to have an American command the operation as a concession. Marshall desired Dwight Eisenhower, a trusted subordinate who was already in Britain as commander of US forces preparing for Roundup.

That should have been the end of it, but it wasn't. At the July 30 JCS meeting, the first chaired by William Leahy, Marshall and King claimed that no definite decision on Gymnast/Torch had been taken until Churchill and Roosevelt expressly abandoned Roundup in favor of it. When FDR was informed of this, he summoned the military chiefs to the White House that same evening to underline that Torch was the 'primary aim' - though he insisted Roundup was still on for 1943, a patent lie that did nothing to convince Marshall of the North African diversion. Rumblings of Torch's persistent opposition made their way into the news as a result of Stimson's leaks. On August 10, Marshall realized things were out of hand when the Secretary of War handed him a draft of a letter he intended to write FDR urging for Torch's cancellation. His refusal to endorse this resulted in the failure of an upcoming rebellion against the commander-in-chief's military judgment.

Only Joseph Stalin could now put a wrench in Torch's plans. He sent Foreign Minister Vyacheslav Molotov to Washington in late May to urge for an early second front to pull off forty German units. As a prelude to the summer onslaught, Case Blue, the Wehrmacht had inflicted two crushing defeats on the Soviets at Kerch and Kharkov, with combined Red Army fatalities exceeding 350,000. Desperate to keep the Soviets in the war, FDR informed Molotov in a White House meeting on May 30 that the US expected a second front in

Europe in 1942, which his military commanders thought improbable. Despite Marshall's vehement protests, he later approved the Foreign Minister's proposed phrase for a public statement stating that there was 'complete understanding' on this point. This was dangerous because it was obvious that Stalin would presume his Anglo-American friends intended to invade France. When he learned that their destination was North Africa, he considered making a separate peace with Hitler.

To avoid this, Winston Churchill traveled to Moscow, accompanied by FDR's emissary, Averell Harriman, for three days of talks in the Kremlin from August 12 to 14. Understandably concerned about the expedition, the prime minister informed FDR, "I feel that things would be easier if we all appeared to be together." I have a difficult job.' Stalin had complete knowledge of the strategic arguments between his friends and knew what was coming because of highly placed spies in London and Washington. On the first day of negotiations, he blamed Churchill for Britain's military failings while complimenting America's fighting capability. When informed the following day about the Torch plan to invade North Africa with 250,000 men, he showed great support for its strategic potential to turn the tide against Germany in the desert war and threaten the Italian heartland. 'May God bless this endeavor,' he said to Churchill and Harriman. Stalin had no illusions that Torch would save the Red Army from a bloodbath in repelling Case Blue, but he recognized its importance in bringing the Americans and British into ground combat with Hitler's forces.

The invasion of North Africa, the most difficult operation of the war thus far, began in the early hours of November 8th. American forces crossing the Atlantic secretly teamed up with British forces to launch a three-pronged assault on Algiers, Casablanca, and Oran. Roosevelt persuaded Churchill to allow US forces to conduct the first landings in the hope of encountering less French resistance, but his optimism was mistaken. Heavy battles in Casablanca and Oran killed 500 Americans and a large number of defenders. Neither the British-backed Free French leader General Charles de Gaulle nor the

American-backed war hero General Henri Giraud, who had escaped from a German prison cell, could persuade their countrymen to lay down their arms. Admiral Jean-Francois Darlan, Vichy's deputy premier and commander-in-chief of its armed forces, was visiting Algiers and was eager to switch sides. On November 10, he consented to a cease-fire that accepted the Allies' right to be in North Africa and kept the Vichy colonial administration in place, with him as High Commissioner.

This was a required agreement with the devil for Torch commander Dwight Eisenhower to induce the French to quit fighting and continue running their colonial lands without the necessity for large-scale Anglo-American occupation. The deal allowed him to concentrate on driving the Germans out of neighboring Tunisia, but putting a renowned Vichy collaborator and anti-Semite in control of ostensibly liberated territory sparked a political firestorm back home. 'Are we fighting Nazis or sleeping with them?' shouted CBS London journalist Ed Murrow. After originally assuring Eisenhower of his full backing, FDR backed down slightly in the face of negative news. On November 17, he said the Darlan accord was a "temporary expedient justified solely by the stress of battle." Darlan's assassination a few weeks later pulled a curtain over the episode, preventing additional embarrassment.

Despite these consequences, FDR had good reason to believe that by the end of 1942, the tide had begun to turn in the struggle against Germany. 'The liberation forces are advancing... to ensure the survival and growth of civilization,' he told an Armistice Day gathering in Arlington. The British Eighth Army's success at El Alamein led Rommel's Afrika Korps into a full retreat from Egypt in the east, shortly before Torch ensconced Anglo-American forces in the west of North Africa. Shortly after, the Red Army surrounded the German Sixth Army in Stalingrad, putting an end to Case Blue's invasion of southern Russia. These accomplishments encouraged Roosevelt to propose a summit meeting in North Africa in early 1943 with Churchill and Stalin to agree on military strategy for the future year and to discuss postwar concerns.

Stalin turned down an invitation to meet in Khartoum, the safest equidistant place for the three, arguing he couldn't leave Russia while the struggle for Stalingrad raged. FDR and Churchill may have met in London to repay the prime minister's transatlantic journeys. The Republicans, revived following a strong showing in the 1942 midterm elections, and their press-baron friends, on the other hand, would have had a field day accusing the president of kowtowing to the British. As a result, FDR chose Casablanca in the North African fighting zone, allowing him to travel as commander-in-chief rather than president and to insist on absolute secrecy in the absence of the media. The voyage offered serious hazards of enemy interception, mishaps, or even assassination, as different advisers reminded her, but Roosevelt paid little attention. The arduous journey began on the evening of January 9 with a two-day train ride from Washington to Miami; from there, a flying boat took the president's party to Trinidad for an overnight stop on 11 January, then on to Belem in Brazil for refueling, followed by an eighteen-hour flight across the Atlantic to Bathurst (now Banjul) in British Gambia on 13 January; and after a night aboard a US warship, the final leg was a Without a doubt, the potential to be the first president to travel by air, the first to leave the country during wartime, and the first since Abraham Lincoln to visit a conflict zone appealed to FDR's love of the dramatic

The first issue to be resolved at the Casablanca discussions was where the Allies would move once the Germans were driven out of North Africa. The American people were divided on this issue. In an early December meeting with Canadian Prime Minister William Mackenzie King at the White House, Roosevelt stated that 'he longed for nothing more than to let the fighting continue in Africa indefinitely' since it was so much easier' to get military supplies to Africa than anywhere else. As a result, well-equipped US forces could gain critical battle experience against the Germans and wear them down via attrition. The tragic raid on Dieppe on 19 August 1942, in which two-thirds of a 5,000-strong Canadian detachment was killed, injured, or captured before even leaving the beaches, strengthened his belief that any effort at a cross-channel invasion of northern France in 1943 would be premature.

When the Joint Chiefs of Staff met with President Franklin D. Roosevelt on January 7, George Marshall urged an amphibious invasion of the Brest peninsula on the Brittany coast, a plan that FDR did not explicitly oppose but regarded even more impracticable than a Normandy operation. After conferring with Allied commanders with Torch experience in Casablanca, the Army Commander changed his mind. The unequivocal assessment of Eisenhower's deputy, General Mark Clark, that a cross-channel assault had little chance of succeeding in 1943 was a particularly critical reality check. Marshall, who had been skeptical about Torch, now saw it as the first of numerous Mediterranean operations that would provide American Marines with the battle experience they required before an amphibious invasion of France in 1944.

FDR was accompanied by a small entourage of advisers, including Harry Hopkins, and the service chiefs (except Leahy, who was left behind in Trinidad suffering from the symptoms of influenza), as well as their senior strategists. Churchill, on the other hand, arrived with a large entourage of staff officers and aides, many of whom could only be accommodated on a cruiser that had participated in the Casablanca landings rather than in venues close to where the negotiations were held. Marshall's chief planner, General Albert Wedemeyer, later complained that the British, by sheer force of numbers, bullied their partners into choosing a Mediterranean strategy rather than a cross-channel route that would have brought the war to a close sooner. He proclaimed, "We came, we listened, and we were conquered." That couldn't be further from the truth. The service chiefs were on the same wavelength as FDR after Marshall spoke with the officers who had participated in Torch. This was confirmed during their meeting on the morning of January 15 in the president's bedroom at his conference mansion, the Villa dar es Saada. In 1943, the United States will, like in the Pacific, adopt an attrition campaign on the outside of enemy lines of communication in the Mediterranean. Once German troops were removed from Tunisia, the next objective would be Sicily, to provide Allied forces experience in amphibious invasion in preparation for the assault on German-held France.

That following day, FDR met with the officer who had led Torch, accompanied by his son and conference aide-de-camp Elliott. Eisenhower had flown from his headquarters in Algiers to go before the CCS for questioning on his failure to seize Tunis at the start of the operation. The British, in particular, held low regard for his military leadership, which was accentuated by irritation that a mere lieutenant general had been granted charge of their more senior forces. Nonetheless, Eisenhower pleased FDR by presenting an honest assessment that it would take until mid-May to dislodge the Germans from Tunisia, where reinforcements had flooded in after the Torch landings. The president also praised his achievement in quickly establishing control of Morocco and Algeria, ensuring that the Allies would not be assaulted on the flank, as Marshall and Stimson had feared.

Encouraged by this experience, Roosevelt intended to conduct a frontal inspection of American troops near the Tunisian border, a plan Marshall flatly rejected as exceedingly hazardous. On the 20th of January, he settled for a very lively day reviewing three divisions of troops stationed near Rabat, about 85 miles northeast of Casablanca. He was driven there with George Patton, who had led the Casablanca landings admirably, and Mark Clark. FDR, seizing the opportunity to be his own intelligence agent, never ceased questioning the generals, impressing them with his inquiring mind. Traveling in an Army jeep for the final stretch caused him excruciating pain, but the resulting photo opportunities fueled patriotic feelings at home. It was the first time an American president has visited American troops on foreign land. Harry Hopkins' son, Robert, an Army combat photographer on the set, was pleased to watch "their jaws drop open " when they recognized who was looking at them. Later, he captured Roosevelt, Clark, and Patton enjoying boiled ham and sweet potatoes with several men. Despite the fact that the guys had no combat experience, FDR was impressed by their passion and commitment. 'Those troops, they truly look like they're rarin' to go,' he told Elliott that evening. Tough, brown, and happy.'

Far less to Roosevelt's liking was his frosty encounter with Charles de Gaulle in the late evening of 22 January. Resentful of being summoned on home soil to see an American president, the Free French leader took further umbrage at FDR's efforts to force him into a shotgun marriage with Giraud to demonstrate their anti-fascist unity under Anglo-American sponsorship. de Gaulle left the meeting with the realization that 'from the moment America entered the war, Roosevelt meant the peace to be an American peace . . . that the states that had been overrun should be subject to his judgment, and that France in particular should recognize him as its savior and arbiter'. Roosevelt, in return, had his suspicions confirmed that de Gaulle wanted to restore French greatness on the back of its empire. The United States, he told Elliott afterwards, was not in the war to resurrect European colonialism. 'When we've won', he avowed, 'I will work with all my might and main to see to it that the United States is not wheedled into the position of accepting any plan that will further France's imperialist ambitions, or that will aid or abet the British empire in its imperial ambitions.'

Unwilling to be party to any foreign intervention in French affairs, de Gaulle refused to sign a conference communiqué of rapprochement with Giraud. He agreed only to be photographed in the garden of Villa dar es Saada shaking hands with his rival in the presence of Churchill and Roosevelt in a public display of supposed unity in front of newsmen gathered there for a press conference. In this case the camera lied because the two Frenchmen remained locked in bitter competition for power in which FDR backed the wrong horse. According to future prime minister Harold Macmillan, on secondment to Eisenhower's staff, de Gaulle was strong, but uncertain. Giraud was reliable but weak.' Exasperated by Giraud's ineptitude, Churchill proposed formal recognition of de Gaulle's French Committee of National Liberation as the provisional government of France in April 1943, which FDR resisted. Eisenhower's support for the British position and de Gaulle's growing popularity with the French people eventually induced the president to back down in August. Roosevelt's determination to prevent France falling back into its sorry pre-war condition caused him to underestimate de Gaulle's vision of restoring its greatness through his own image of indomitability. As British foreign secretary Anthony Eden observed, FDR 'wanted to hold the strings of France's future in his own hands'.

The de Gaulle–Giraud handshake would have been a memorable way of ending the Casablanca talks but FDR trumped it in the news conference that followed. The fifty correspondents in attendance were amazed to learn that he had been conferring with Churchill for the last ten days without their knowledge. To the consternation of Propaganda Minister Joseph Goebbels, the Nazis only learned of the talks when the main story given the newsmen hit the headlines. This was Roosevelt's announcement that the Anglo-American allies were in agreement that the elimination of Axis war power was the only way to ensure world peace. The unconditional surrender of Germany, Japan and Italy to the United Nations was essential to that end. Its attainment, FDR was careful to emphasize, required the destruction not of their peoples but of 'the philosophies in those countries which are based on conquest and the subjugation of other people'.

After the war, many criticized the unconditional surrender statement for inciting Germany and Japan to fight to the bitter end. The New York Times' military editor, Hanson Baldwin, called it a big blunder for inciting "unconditional resistance." It was perceived as a spur-of-the-moment move thrown on FDR's allies and advisors without input. Churchill later claimed that he had no previous knowledge of the news conference. Similarly, Albert Wedemeyer claimed that if the service chiefs had been questioned, they would have counseled against demanding unconditional surrender for fear of prolonging the war by removing the enemy's desire to discuss peace.

FDR had appraised the JCS of his thinking in their White House meeting on 7 January 1943, and there had been no opposition in response. He had also obtained Churchill's enthusiastic endorsement for the strategy over a private luncheon at his conference villa on the 18th of January, a decision that was conveyed with the CCS later that afternoon. The prime minister immediately cabled his War Cabinet to declare his consent for a declaration of clear intention' that the Anglo-American allies will 'continue the war mercilessly until we have achieved the "unconditional surrender" of Germany and Japan. On January 21, that body formally accepted the policy.

FDR was undoubtedly a driving force behind the establishment of 'unconditional surrender' as Anglo-American policy. He was adamant that no Great War-style armistice would be used by another Hitler as a stab in the back betrayal of Germany. According to Robert Sherwood, FDR "wanted to ensure that when the war was won, it would stay won." In the absence of a second front in Europe, the president sought to reassure Stalin that his Anglo-American allies would never negotiate a separate peace with Hitler.75 Roosevelt was aware that it had the potential to prolong the war, although none of his later detractors offered solid proof of this. The leaders of Germany and Japan, militaristic, fanatical, and fascist, realized that a peace negotiated from a position of increasing weakness beginning in 1943 would have meant their death just as assuredly as unconditional surrender.

Roosevelt's call for unconditional surrender signaled the beginning of a new phase in the war. For the majority of 1942, the United States, Britain, and the Soviet Union were fighting a defensive war against Nazi Germany. The Japanese evacuation from Corregidor, which occurred shortly after FDR and Churchill departed Casablanca, verified the same turning point in the Pacific war. The strategic leadership of Roosevelt was critical to these developments. By opposing his service commanders and their Cabinet partner, Henry Stimson, against early cross-channel operations, he had protected the Anglo-American alliance's Europe-first policy and saved it from a shattering setback that could have jeopardized the alliance's final victory over Hitler. In mid-February 1943, Rommel's stunning victory over a corps of Eisenhower's tank and infantry forces at Kasserine Pass, Tunisia, indicated that American leaders and troops needed more battle experience before they were ready for more dangerous situations. Roosevelt also created the groundwork for primacy in his 1942 collaboration with Churchill. Resistance to early cross-channel operations had put him on the same page as the prime minister, making the Casablanca strategy appear to be a victory for British interests. As the year continued, the reality of FDR's dominance became clear in conflicts over military priorities beyond the Mediterranean theater.

9

Commander-in-chief

Arsenals and alliances

In a December 1940 Fireside Chat, FDR urged America to be the "great arsenal of democracy" in order to get support for the Lend-Lease program that Congress would soon adopt. The designation was meant to imply that sending war equipment to countries battling Germany would avoid America from having to send its own sons into battle. Roosevelt gave the United States new meaning when it became belligerent. 'We cannot outfight our adversaries unless we also outproduce them,' he declared in his 1942 budget presentation to Congress. 'We must vastly outproduce them, so that there is no doubt about our ability to offer devastating supremacy in any theater of the world war.' These statements, which perfectly encapsulated FDR's knowledge that America was fighting a GNP war, preceded his proposal for a war budget of $53 billion in FY1943, more than double the level in FY1942.

'The advantage of the United Nations in armaments and ships must be overwhelming - so overwhelming that the Axis Nations can never expect to catch up with it,' Roosevelt said in the next day's State of the Union Address. We have the capability and capacity to manufacture weaponry not only for our own forces, but also for armies, navies, and air forces fighting alongside us.' He then outlined increased war production targets for 1942, as well as predicted increases for 1943, including 60,000 planes increasing to 125,000, 45,000 tanks increasing to 75,000, 20,000 anti-aircraft guns increasing to 35,000, and 6 million deadweight tons of commerce shipping increasing to 10 million. 'Roosevelt stunned us,' said Donald Nelson, a prominent officer in defense mobilization. 'No one in our production team thought this volume was possible.' Undaunted by their doubts, FDR told Lend-Lease chief Harry Hopkins, 'Oh, the production folks can accomplish it if they really try.'

FDR broadcast these aims in order to bolster public morale at a time when the war was going badly. 'It was in Roosevelt's tendency to believe that the surest way to capture the imagination of the American people was to give them the greatest possible task,' speechwriter Robert Sherwood remarked. He was also conducting psychological warfare to scare the Axis countries about the size of America's productive capacity. In his reasoning, there was also a deeper strategic rationale. Roosevelt was well aware of America's distinct advantage over the other main belligerents in being able to wage a war of machines rather than troops. The role of 'arsenal of democracy' permitted the US to take the shortest path to victory, leaving much of the real fighting to its allies, most notably the Soviet Union. This reduced the possibility of incurring significant losses, which may rekindle popular hostility to America becoming extensively involved in international affairs once peace was restored. It also promised to place the United States in an unrivaled position of economic supremacy in the postwar world. 'That vision may not have been fully formed in Roosevelt's mind in early 1942, but it was consistent with his policies during the neutrality period, and its possibilities were latent both in the military strategy he adopted and in the mobilization program he outlined,' historian David Kennedy observed.

Despite taking longer than any other industrial nation to fully recover from the Great Depression, America was an economic behemoth, accounting for one-fifth of global income in 1938, far more than Germany, Italy, and Japan combined. With over nine million unemployed and vast swaths of idle industrial plants in 1940, it had enormous spare capacity to enhance military production in the eighteen months before Pearl Harbor. Self-sufficiency in several raw materials, most notably a three-fifths share of global oil production, and physical security were also advantages. Despite these advantages, the United States encountered difficulties in transitioning its economy to a full war footing.

The difficulty in getting the all-important steel industry, which is the key underpinning for military manufacturing, to optimize output during the neutrality period foreshadowed the difficulties that lay ahead. Though liberals perceived steel executives preferring scarcity to enhance prices and profits, steel executives were more concerned with not being left with surplus capacity once the defense crisis passed. As one of those involved in the effort, economist John Kenneth Galbraith, put it, the president and his staff used carrots and sticks to "get [them] off their asses." The administration relaxed antitrust laws, accelerated tax write-offs for investment, and threatened to encourage new entrants into the sector, most notably Henry Kaiser, all of which secured industry agreement in 1941 to expand basic capacity by 13 million tons.

Once America was at war, FDR had to build an effective economic mobilization machinery nearly from scratch. The agencies created during the neutrality period, particularly the Office of Production Management, were unfit for purpose. As with the New Deal, Roosevelt established a slew of new bodies, many with limited or overlapping responsibilities, that provided him executive authority to settle conflicts. The War Production Board (WPB), established in February 1942, was far from the mobilization superagency that its moniker implied. Other bodies, numbering at least a dozen in total, were given control over areas such as labor, manpower, and prices. The WPB also did not seize control of contract distribution from military procurement authorities that preferred to deal directly with regular suppliers.

Many enterprises were slow to shift to war production since defense jobs increased consumer spending until the WPB imposed restrictions on non-essential manufacturing in mid-1942. This did not address the need for plant construction to satisfy Roosevelt's targets. Corporations remained wary of investing in new facilities that might become unprofitable once the conflict ended. As a result, similar to steel, the federal government underwrote the majority of the development expenditures, awarded cost-plus-fixed-fee contracts to ensure profitability, and abandoned anti-monopoly laws. These incentives produced additional challenges of unfettered business competition for scarce raw commodities such as copper, steel, and aluminum. The Controlled Materials Plan, which went into full effect in mid-1943, eventually required all procurement agencies to estimate their commodity needs for WPB allocation determination. Meanwhile, in previously underdeveloped industrial areas, particularly the Pacific West and the South, inadequate housing, transportation, and public amenities posed a threat to major industry production. In April 1943, Roosevelt established the Committee for Congested Production Areas under the Executive Office of the Presidency to coordinate the many agencies dealing with labor-supply issues.

Jurisdictional disputes among the intricate web of agencies participating in economic mobilization were unavoidable, but one in particular stood out for its high-profile squabbling. When the WPB proposed the Controlled Materials Plan in late 1942, it sparked a "public "knock-down and drag-out" dispute with the military, which demanded complete control over procurement, according to Budget Director Harold Smith. FDR considered firing WPB chief Donald Nelson, enraged that press reports of the disagreement contradicted his rhetoric of a united war effort. Smith, on the other hand, persuaded him that the problem was a "lack of unity, vigor, and definite policy" caused by the agency's structural inability to coordinate the production hierarchy. As a result, Roosevelt established a new agency, the Office of Economic Stabilization, led by his one-time political fixer, James Byrnes, to fulfill that duty.

After leaving the Supreme Court, which he referred to as the "marble mausoleum," Byrnes was eager to return to the political front lines as the official tasked with resolving the alleged disaster in Washington. 'It's simply not possible for me to devote enough time to domestic concerns,' the president reportedly told him. 'All of these new agencies... entail an increase in the amount of jurisdictional conflicts that come before me for resolution. I want you to resolve those disagreements for me; I'll issue an executive order granting you the authority to do so, and I'll make it clear that your decision is my decision.' This meant that Byrnes would essentially be the Assistant President. Anyone so labeled by the press during the New Deal era was fired by a president envious of his power, but FDR suddenly acknowledged that coordination of economic mobilization required just such a lieutenant.

In May 1943, Byrnes was promoted to lead the Office of War Mobilization (OWM), a new agency situated atop the administrative hierarchy of the Executive Office of the President. WPB boss and former Sears Roebuck chairman Donald Nelson humorously recalled Roosevelt telling him that businesses attracted to the government 'don't know how to administer the things they must administer as well as politicians know how'. Byrnes, who was well-versed in the ways of Washington, intuitively recognized that his duty was to be FDR's home-front troubleshooter. As OHM's leader, he prioritized resolving disagreements as they arose rather than taking on operational or long-term planning responsibilities. His success was founded not on considerable organizational innovation, but on political acumen, proximity to FDR, and a rejection of mission creep. When Roosevelt asked another of his political fixers, Samuel Rosenman, to examine the need for OHM's establishment, he concluded, "Jimmy is the perfect man for the job." The setup will function... and free you up to spend the majority of your time fighting the war and planning for "after the war."

Almost as soon as OWM was established, the president was forced to settle a public fight between two government titans too large for Byrnes to handle. A long-simmering feud between Vice President Henry Wallace and Secretary of Commerce Jesse Jones erupted in June 1943. Wallace, as head of the Board of Economic Warfare, accused Jones of neglecting to acquire stockpiles of critical resources during the neutrality period and then blocking his agency's efforts to obtain them, claims that Jones regarded as malicious. FDR, who was notoriously sluggish to settle disputes among New Deal subordinates, did not tolerate wartime squabbles. He abruptly informed the feuding duo that their 'unfortunate disagreement and contentious public debate' necessitated the transfer of responsibility for the matters at hand to other hands. There was no time to evaluate the veracity of their opposing claims in the midst of a fight deemed "critical to our national security and the future of civilization." The main goal was to "clear the decks and get on with the war" with "new men, free of interagency dissension and bitterness." FDR fired Wallace's agency and put Byrnes in charge of its replacement, the Office of Economic Warfare (OEW), which also took over elements of Jones' bureaucratic empire. To avoid such public squabbles, the president informed every department and agency leader that anyone who aired grievances in the press would be fired immediately. This lightning strike ended public wrangling but not behind-the-scenes squabbling between opposing officials.

Despite hitches in mobilization, the United States easily won the war of machines. Between 1941 and 1945, it produced 8,812 significant naval warships, much outnumbering Britain's 951 and Japan's 538. Equally vital, the 5,000 commercial boats launched from its shipyards kept Britain and Russia's supply routes open. The 90,000 landing craft made in the United States were critical to Allied amphibious operations. Meanwhile, the United States manufactured 306,181 aircraft, considerably outnumbering the Soviet, British, and German totals of 137,271, 108,560, and 99,339, respectively. The Allies received a quarter of all wartime supplies, more than half of all Red Army motorized vehicles, and 90% of UK and Soviet aviation fuel at an octane grade far higher than Germany could refine. America developed a 1,400-mile pipeline from Texas to Pennsylvania and a large fleet of tankers with an aggregate weight of 11.4 million by 1945, up from 2.5 million in 1941.

To witness the manufacturing miracle for himself, Roosevelt embarked on an unprecedented tour of twenty-six defense industries and military bases in September 1942, which included an 8,750-mile train journey across America. Donald Nelson's pre-trip briefing did not prepare him for the magnitude of what he witnessed. This was only realized during the first stops, which included the new Chrysler Tank Factory in Detroit, which was producing thirty tanks per day, and the new Ford factory at Willow Run, where the world's first mass-production assembly line would eventually produce B-24 Liberator bombers at a rate of one every sixty-three minutes. The journey continued west to the Boeing aviation plant in Seattle, where weekly output of sixty B-17 Flying Fortresses would nearly double by the conclusion of the war. The tour's highlight was watching the launch of a 10,000-ton freighter built in just ten days at the Kaiser shipyard in Portland. Roosevelt was then driven around the shops fabricating vessel sections to be welded into place on the slipway. This prefabrication technology, the invention of Henry Kaiser, a corporate enthusiast for all-out manufacturing, enabled the yard to turn out ships at previously unimaginable speed. Roosevelt then visited the Mare Island Navy Yard outside Oakland, which specialized in submarine construction and repair, as well as the Douglas aircraft complex in Los Angeles. On the way back east, he passed by another B-24 mass-production plant in Fort Worth, Texas, and the Higgins boatyard in New Orleans, which was revolutionizing the production of landing craft that would play a critical part in amphibious operations in Europe and the Pacific. The tour verified FDR's vision of America becoming an industrial titan with nearly inconceivable potential for producing war materials had become a reality.

Big business's prestige had plunged with the economy in the gloomy 1930s, but wartime manufacturing marvels rebuilt its image. Unemployment fell from 14.6% of the labor force in 1940 to 1.2% in 1944, workers in manufacturing saw a 27% real increase in income between 1940 and 1945 (due primarily to overtime), and economic output increased by 52% in inflation-adjusted terms from 1939 to 1944. Military-related output increased from 2% of GNP in 1939 to 40% of GNP in 1943, hastening the emergence of corporate oligopoly. Between 1941 and 1945, more than two-thirds of primary military contracts were awarded to just 100 companies, with the 33 largest corporations receiving more than half of them - General Motors led the way with a 10% share of total war output. In the view of procurement officials, this select band possessed the qualities of dependability, efficiency, and familiarity.

Profitability and patriotism were inextricably linked for big industry, as post-tax corporate profits soared from $6.4 billion in 1940 to $11 billion in 1944. When peace was restored, the corporate sector received a huge boost when only 87 companies purchased nearly two-thirds of the $17 billion in government-financed plants and equipment being offered at rock-bottom prices. The conflict had established the groundwork for what became known as the "military-industrial complex," a cartelistic alliance between the armed forces and big business that was at the heart of the Cold conflict state. Secretary of War Henry Stimson said in 1940, 'If you are going to go to war, or prepare for war, in a capitalist society, you have to let business earn money out of the process, or business will not work.' If FDR was indifferent about the increasing concentration of military production, he was more willing to fight for a fair tax structure to fund the war. In 1939, just four million Americans were required to file personal income tax returns, the majority of whom were subject to the basic rate of 4%. Because their annual earnings fell below the basic exemption amount of $1,500, the remaining working population did not pay any federal income tax. The Income Tax Act of 1942 changed the income tax from an elite levy to a mass tax. It reduced the personal exemption rate to $624 in order to drain inflationary purchasing power, bringing thirteen million new taxpayers into the rolls. By 1945, wartime prosperity had expanded the taxation base even further, with 42.6 million Americans (essentially three-quarters of all employees) paying income taxes at basic rates of 6% and marginal rates ranging up to 94% for high earners. Individuals paid more in aggregate taxes than corporations for the first time, creating a long-term trend. They also made monthly contributions at work beginning in 1943, thanks to the new withholding system that made companies liable for deducting taxes from their employees' pay packets.

Ordinary Americans acclimated to the new tax structure with amazing tolerance, but industry wanted a hard line drawn against more charges. In reaction to corporate lobbying, conservative Democrats and Republicans balked at FDR's call for a new tax to raise $10.5 billion for the war effort in late 1943. They passed a substitute bill that raised barely $2 billion while providing special-interest tax breaks. FDR vetoed it, saying, 'The responsibility of the Congress of the United States is to supply the Government of the United States as a whole with adequate revenue for wartime needs, to provide fiscal support for the stabilization program, to hold firm against the tide of special privileges, and to achieve real simplicity for millions of small income taxpayers.' Long-time Roosevelt friend Alben Barkley (D-Kentucky) resigned as Senate Majority Leader in protest of what he saw as an assault on his own and Congress's integrity, but was re-elected overwhelmingly. The House and Senate both voted by significant numbers to override FDR, turning the issue into one of congressional dignity rather than tax fairness. This was the first time the legislature overrode the president's veto of a revenue bill. Seeing no use in pursuing an unwinnable conflict, Roosevelt settled for a private tirade against the "very small number of people who would rather nail my hide to the barn door than win the war."

The United States paid for 45 percent of total war costs through taxes, a far smaller share than its economy could have supported. The remainder came via the sale of approximately $200 billion in Treasury bonds, roughly a quarter of which were purchased by individuals and the remainder by banks and other financial organizations. In 1942, purchasing agencies began awarding military contracts without regard for the economy's ability to meet them. This sparked the so-called Feasibility Dispute between the WPB and the military over procurement speed and magnitude. By the end of the year, the Joint Chiefs of Staff had grudgingly determined that there was a major mismatch between the economy's productive capacity and excessive military demand. They decided to cut $13 billion from purchasing plans, delay manufacturing timelines, and lower expected ground-force enlistment by 300,000.

The Feasibility Dispute combined with two other developments to have a significant impact on American strategic theory. The US Army's Eighth Air Force launched its first bombing operation on continental Europe on August 17, 1942, destroying rail yards near Rouen in northern France. The mission prompted air-power supporters to argue that its widespread use was critical to Germany's defeat. Within a few months, the impending loss of Hitler's forces on the other side of the continent in the Battle of Stalingrad put an end to any misgivings about the Soviet ability to fight on. The US war plan was initially based on the Victory Program's 1941 assumption that Hitler's invasion would force Russia out of the war. When Germany no longer had to worry about the eastern front, military planners projected that America would need a massive force of 213 divisions to successfully invade Western Europe. Such calculations were rendered outdated by the events of Rouen and Stalingrad. Army estimates of future manpower needs were reduced to 125 divisions, then 100, and finally 90 divisions in July 1943, reflecting the economic constraints exposed by the Feasibility Dispute.

The revised Victory Program Troop Basis, dubbed the "90-Division Gamble," obtained FDR's formal assent as commander-in-chief in November 1943. It represented his 'arsenal of democracy' idea, as updated in the 1942 State of the Union Address. According to military historian Maurice Matloff, American strategic doctrine accepted a new gospel that 'the single greatest tangible advantage that the United States provided to the coalition in World War II was the production power of its industry' from then on. A 90-division Army established a compromise in military planners' calculations between the minimal strength required to win the war and the maximum number of personnel that could be inducted without overstretching the resources of war industries that held the key to victory. They believed that a smaller ground force, backed by an overwhelming preponderance of armament and technology, would be sufficient to wage a modern war of mobility. As a result, by the end of 1943, the United States had amassed an arsenal that provided Allied forces a three-to-one weapons advantage over their adversaries in the year's major operations. To compensate for a lesser army, it constructed a vast air force capable of raining down unprecedentedly damaging bombs on enemy territory.

In August 1945, two atomic bombs were dropped on the Japanese cities of Hiroshima and Nagasaki, thus ending the war. When warned of the hazards of Germany winning the race to build weapons of mass destruction, FDR sanctioned their development nearly six years earlier. In the pre-war period, a group of scientists, many of whom were Jewish immigrants, were unable to warn the military bureaucracy about this menace. They eventually expressed their worries in a letter to FDR, which was signed by the eminent émigré physicist Albert Einstein and personally handed to the president by economist Alexander Sachs on October 11, 1939. With his eyes opened to the danger, Roosevelt established the Advisory Committee on Uranium, which met for the first time on October 21 but made little headway in overcoming the enormous scientific obstacles of actually building a bomb.

The Office of Scientific Research and Development was founded inside the EOP's Office of Emergency Management in June 1941 to coordinate atomic research under the supervision of Vannevar Bush of the Carnegie Institution, who reported only to FDR. The revelation by the British that a few kilograms of plutonium, a man-made uranium, could cause an atomic explosion prompted Bush to seek presidential authorization for a full-scale American attempt to develop the A-bomb. He cautioned in a briefing report that the costs would be exorbitant. On 19 January 1942, Roosevelt gave the go-ahead in uncommonly harsh terms: 'OK - returned - 'I believe you should keep this in your own safe.' This started in motion the process through which the Manhattan Project would spend over $2 billion before successfully testing an atomic weapon in the New Mexico desert on July 16, 1945.

According to Harvard's James Conant, a prominent presidential adviser on atomic development, Roosevelt did not grasp the revolutionary significance of the new weaponry, and hence "the program never got very far beyond the threshold of his consciousness." In actuality, the president was instrumental in keeping the project continuing during severe funding and material shortages in 1943. He paid only occasional attention to developments on a weapon whose development was far from guaranteed, but he did not dismiss the potential that it would become a reality in time. Winston Churchill felt enraged over the issue of notifying the Russians about the atomic project. Despite agreeing to the prime minister's demand that the new weapon be kept in Anglo-American hands, he kept his options open in practice. FDR also refused to commit to using the bomb if it was created during the war. In the expectation that Germany would have been defeated by then, he agreed with Churchill at Hyde Park in September 1944 that it might perhaps, after mature consideration, be used against the Japanese, who should be warned that this bombardment will be repeated until they surrender'.

While US manufacturing was critical to the Grand Alliance's military success, Roosevelt's leadership was as important as the political pivot for the alliance's advance toward victory. Obtaining Churchill's support for an Anglo-American cross-channel invasion of France was his most difficult task in keeping the Big Three together. The establishment of this second front was critical in gaining Joseph Stalin's assent to enter the war against Japan once Germany was beaten, as well as to ensure ongoing Great Power collaboration during peacetime. Although the Roosevelt-Churchill partnership is remembered as the cornerstone of the Anglo-American special relationship, FDR was considerably more interested in cultivating excellent connections with the Soviet leader, whose support he saw as necessary for establishing a lasting peace. In his opinion, Britain's early wartime catastrophes in Western Europe, North Africa, and Southeast Asia had damaged its mentality and depleted its vigor. He allegedly told Vice President Henry Wallace, "The United States and Russia are young powers, and England is an old, tired power." According to his vision, the new world order that arose from the global conflict would have to be based on the Soviet-American entente.

Though FDR claimed to despise communism just as much as fascism, he worked hard to maintain a positive relationship with his Russian counterpart. Stalin, a member of the collective leadership that gained control of the Soviet Union in 1924, solidified his influence into dictatorship in the 1930s. In that function, he had a harsh track record of forced collectivization at exorbitant human costs, as well as indiscriminate purges to eliminate up to a million alleged adversaries. Roosevelt made it his job to learn everything he could about Stalin, and while he had no illusions about his ruthlessness, he believed him 'gettable' (a term Harry Hopkins used after meeting him for the first time in 1941). He tried to persuade Stalin that a mutually guaranteed peace by the Great Powers was the required foundation for Russia's postwar economic modernisation. FDR informed his personal physician, Vice Admiral Ross McIntire, "I bank on his realism." 'He's probably sick of sitting on bayonets.' Daisy Suckley, Roosevelt's close companion, wrote in her diary a week after his death of Roosevelt's confidence that the Soviet leader would work with him to build the peace: 'F. himself did not have too much faith in Stalin, but he thought that he & Stalin looked at things in the same practical way, & that for that reason, there was much hope that Stalin would follow along.'

Stalin, a communist theorist, was intensely distrustful of the capitalist West and its political leaders. Roosevelt, well aware of this, made every attempt to gain his trust. He was adamant about meeting all of Stalin's supply requests for feeding, clothing, and arming Russian forces, even if it meant jeopardizing America's own war effort. To that aim, the Hopkins-led Soviet Protocol Committee signed a series of annual agreements outlining the United States' supply. Because of the U-boat menace in the North Atlantic, the quickest supply route from New York to Archangel was also the most dangerous. Despite severe losses sustained by American convoys, FDR kept a careful check on progress in maintaining protocol-agreed quotas and communicated his displeasure to the US Maritime Commissioner if supply rates fell behind. In March 1942, he issued a directive to all US agencies involved in Lend-Lease that meeting their obligations to the Soviet Union came first.

For Stalin, the early formation of a second front through the Anglo-American invasion of France was the major litmus test for the trustworthiness of his allies. Strategic harmony was difficult to obtain for the United States and the United Kingdom on this score. American service chiefs wished to finish the European war as soon as possible by directing overwhelming Allied power on Hitler. The British, on the other hand, favored an indirect approach of bombing, embargo, and peripheral military actions on multiple fronts to bring Germany to its knees. Their skepticism about the possibility of direct conquest was heightened by memories of the Great War bloodshed and the military failures of 1940-2. Britain also sought to prioritize operations in areas advantageous to its imperial objectives, such as the Mediterranean, the Balkans, and the Middle East in the European theater, and Southeast Asia in the Far East.

As his support for Operation Torch revealed, FDR stood in the middle of his service leaders and the British in terms of how to destroy Germany. Before undertaking the risky invasion of northern France, he wanted to ensure that American generals and men had experience battling Hitler's battle-hardened troops in a secondary theater. He accepted the British advice at the Casablanca meeting that Sicily be the next objective when the Germans were driven out of North Africa. There were good reasons for this: possession of the island's air bases put southern Italy within range of bomber raids that could undermine Mussolini's now-teetering regime, and if a new Italian government appeared likely to surrender, Hitler would have to withdraw some of his forces from the eastern front to shore up his southern flank.

The Sicilian campaign, which began on July 10, 1943 and ended on August 17, 1943, taught Allied commanders significant lessons in intelligence gathering, deception tactics, integrated US-UK leadership, and air-, naval-, and ground-force coordination. On July 19, an American force of nearly 500 B-17s and B-24s launched the war's greatest air raid against Rome's railway marshaling yards and neighboring airfields. It resulted in the toppling of Il Duce on July 25, paving the way for Italy's acceptance of an armistice on

September 3. The first schism in the Axis collaboration highlighted Anglo-American fault lines, urging Churchill to seek the Mediterranean-Balkan road to Hitler's demise rather than the cross-channel option.

At the Trident summit in Washington DC in mid-May 1943, Americans and British argued on war strategy. In order to prepare for a cross-channel assault in 1944, Roosevelt stipulated unambiguously that Mediterranean operations be limited once Sicily was conquered. Churchill, on the other hand, planned to knock Italy out of the war and then proceed on German-held territory in the Balkans, where he believed a successful campaign would entice Turkey to join the Allies. Gnawing at Nazi Germany's vulnerable underbelly was expected to drive it to the brink of collapse, allowing a cross-channel operation to give the coup de grace. The British insisted that the Allies lacked the strength to launch an invasion of France in 1944, where twenty-five German divisions stood poised to fight them. General Alan Brooke stated at a meeting of the Combined Chiefs of Staff (CCS) that 'no actions would be conceivable until 1945 or 1946, since it must be remembered that in past conflicts there had always been some 80 French divisions available on our side.' After days of wrangling, the military chiefs agreed that once Sicily was secured, major offensive operations could be carried out to tie down the relatively small number of German divisions in Italy for the remainder of the summer months before the most experienced US and UK divisions were transferred to Britain to prepare for the invasion of France in May 1944, now code-named Overlord. For George Marshall, this was an essential compromise in order to sustain coalition combat, but he was concerned that if Hitler opted to rebuild his army in Italy, Allied operations would become "extremely difficult and time consuming."

If the new invasion schedule was a year or more too soon for British tastes, it was a year too late for Russians. In March 1943, Stalin wrote to FDR that Hitler's anticipated summer attack made it "particularly important for us that the blow from the West be no longer delayed, that it be delivered this spring or in early summer."

In an attempt to reconcile problems, Roosevelt dispatched Joseph Davies to Moscow in early May with a personal invitation to meet on either side of the Bering Strait between Russia and Alaska. Davies had a good relationship with Stalin when serving as ambassador to Moscow from 1936 to 1938, and he was an essential source of advice for FDR on the necessity for huge aid to keep Russia in the war. As a result, he was the ideal conduit to carry out Roosevelt's intention, as revealed to Daisy Suckley, "to talk, man to man, with Stalin, and try to establish a constructive relationship."

FDR, according to speechwriter Samuel Rosenman, "was firmly convinced of his own ability to get along with people and work out acceptable agreements with them." Though he had never met Stalin, FDR felt confident that he would fare better dealing with him alone, without the constraints of Churchill's staunch anti-communism. 'I know you won't mind me being brutally honest when I tell you that I think I can personally handle Stalin better than either your Foreign Office or my State Department,' he had written to the prime minister in early 1942. Stalin despises the guts of all your top officials. He likes me more now, and I hope he continues to do so.' Of course, Churchill was concerned because he worried his two allies would negotiate an arrangement over which he would have no influence. Fortunately for him, Stalin first saw his Anglo-American rivals as speaking in unison, and hence considered them both equally responsible for delaying a cross-channel invasion while Russia bled dry battling Germany.

Joseph Davies returned from Moscow with the Soviet leader's promise to meet on or around July 15 in Fairbanks, Alaska, and a clear warning of his expectations. 'Stalin,' he reported to FDR on June 2,'said to me directly that he could accept neither the African invasion nor the Air Attack on Germany as a Second Front.... He was skeptical, not only of the British, but of us as well.' A furious Stalin despatched identical cables to Roosevelt and Churchill upon receiving formal notification of the Trident schedule for Overlord, accusing them of violating their vow to open a second front in 1943. Their choice forced the Red Army, "fighting not only for its country, but also for its Allies," to "do the job alone, almost single-handedly, against an enemy that is still very strong and formidable." The telegram concluded on a foreboding note, stating that the Soviet Union would be unable to accept a decision made "without its participation and without any attempt at a joint discussion of this highly important matter, which may gravely affect the subsequent course of the war." This letter, in whatever interpretation, indicated that the scheduled Roosevelt-Stalin discussions were doomed. Worryingly, it aroused doubts about the Grand Alliance's ability to stick together long enough to defeat Hitler, let alone construct a lasting peace.

'It was lucky that Hitler did not know how poor relations were between the Allies at that period, how near they were to the disruption that was his only hope,' said Robert Sherwood. The German discovery in April 1943 of mass graves in the Katyn Forest of nearly 22,000 Polish army commanders, police officials, and intellectuals slain in cold blood by Soviet occupation forces in 1940 complicated efforts to maintain Allied unity. Stalin severed ties with the Polish government-in-exile in London after it demanded an International Red Cross investigation, blaming the Nazis for the slaughter. FDR argued politely but in vain that "with several million Poles in the United States," such action "would not help the current situation." Despite obvious evidence of Soviet guilt, he prioritized sustaining Big Three unity over condemning Stalin's moral reprehensibility. The only way Roosevelt could gain leverage with his Russian friend was to put Anglo-American troops on the ground in France, but Churchill now believed that the Mediterranean-Balkan path was the only way into Eastern Europe before the Red Army could conquer it.

When the prime minister returned from Trident, he began to backtrack on Overlord. Secretary of War Henry Stimson was astonished to discover Churchill enthusiastic about operations in Italy as the first phase in his own victory strategy while visiting Britain to review the US build-up for the cross-channel invasion. 'We cannot now realistically hope,' he told FDR, 'to be able to cross the

Channel and confront our German adversary under a British commander.' According to him, the shadows of Passchendaele and Dunkerque still hang too heavily over Churchill and his generals for their hearts to be in Overlord. 'The difference between us,' he continued, 'is a basic difference of faith.' This was the last thing Roosevelt needed to hear after receiving Stalin's proposal for a Big Three summit in late 1943. As a result, it was critical for the Anglo-American allies to demonstrate a unified commitment to Overlord. As a result, Roosevelt hoped to settle second-front issues once and for all at the Quadrant negotiations in Quebec, which were originally scheduled for September but were pushed back to mid-August due to the quickly changing situation in Italy.

At a meeting at the White House on August 10, the president and his military commanders agreed that there would be no Balkan campaign, that Overlord would proceed as planned, and that the Americans would provide the majority of the soldiers for the invasion to assure that one of their own would command. FDR was adamant that "our preponderance of force should be sufficient to render it impossible for the British to disagree." He was willing to give a bone to Churchill by agreeing to cooperate operations in Italy as long as they did not go beyond Rome. During an earlier meeting with FDR, George Marshall expressed worry that a multi-front strategy would divert scarce resources away from Overlord. This word of warning was met with the breezy comment that military planners were 'always conservative and saw all the problems, and that more could typically be done than they were ready to concede'. Roosevelt believed that the American people, like Stalin, would not accept nine months of no serious ground-force involvement against the Germans in the run-up to Overlord.

To create the groundwork for Quadrant, FDR called Churchill to a pre-conference retreat at Hyde Park, where they resolved two critical alliance business problems. The prime minister had long protested that America had broken its agreement to share atomic research with Britain, which Roosevelt had now reiterated. In turn, the president forced Churchill to accept an American commander of Overlord on the basis that the US would contribute the most personnel and materials to the venture. This amounted to public acknowledgement that the United States had become the alliance's senior partner, restricting Britain's ability to postpone Overlord. There is little indication that sharing atomic research was a trade-off, but Churchill must have realized that failing to meet the cross-channel commitment meant losing access. As a result, the Quebec conference validated the key conclusions taken at Hyde Park and authorized continued operations in Italy subject to non-diversion of resources from Overlord.

This arrangement did not put Churchill's prospect of achieving his strategic vision to rest, but its stupidity was swiftly exposed. On hearing of the Anglo-American landings in Sicily, Hitler abruptly ended the Kursk offensive in western Russia and sent significant reinforcements to secure his position in Italy. Though it never regained its offensive impetus in Russia - or anyplace else - the Wehrmacht remained quite capable of fighting defensive war on multiple fronts. Hitler adjusted his military strategy to account for this new reality. According to him, German forces could still hold the line on the eastern front, maintain the Atlantic Wall in the west, and contain Anglo-American operations in the south. German troops seized control of Italy's industrial north and displaced the country's occupying forces in the Balkans and the Aegean. After negotiations with Hitler, Joseph Goebbels stated, "The fundamental principle of our war strategy is to keep the war as far away from the borders of the homeland as possible." In fact, it was already there in the skies, as proved by UK and US air force raids on Hamburg in late July, which killed around 37,000 people. Nonetheless, Hitler remained optimistic that the longer the ground conflict dragged on without a settlement, the more likely it was that either the Soviets or the Anglo-Americans would seek a separate peace. The Red Army's success in moving beyond the Dnieper in the autumn to seize Ukraine's bountiful granaries and the northern Caucasus industrial heartlands did not dampen this optimism. Goebbels wrote in his notebook, 'There is only one possibility for our adversaries to secure total triumph in this war, and that is a successful invasion of the West.'

The Anglo-American allies' post-Sicily floundering posed little threat to the Third Reich. On September 9, their amphibious invasion of mainland Italy came dangerously close to failing to establish its Salerno beachhead. Creating a pattern for the entire campaign, a combination of insufficient resources, poor command coordination, bad field decisions, and fierce German defense shattered overconfident expectations of an easy advance from there to Naples, which was not taken until 1 October - and only then because Hitler's forces retreated to make a stand just north of the city. Meanwhile, Churchill sought to capitalize on Italy's surrender by seizing control of the Dodecanese islands in the southeast Aegean. The Germans beat him to one of their final great triumphs of the war. In a disastrous attempt to seize Rhodes and neighboring isles, the British lost 1,500 troops dead, 3,000 captured, 8 vessels sunk and several more heavily damaged, and 113 aircraft destroyed due to a lack of appropriate air cover. Churchill reluctantly called off the plan after the Americans refused to shift resources from Overlord to bail him out. Roosevelt had advocated securing "whatever hold we could in the Dodecanese without heavy commitment," but the situation had altered. 'Strategically,' he told Churchill, 'if we capture the Aegean Islands, I wonder where we go from there, and vice versa, where would the Germans go if they retained possession of the Islands for some time?'

Rather than suffocating Churchill's fixation with the Mediterranean theater, Roosevelt's response fueled his determination to derail its resource-guzzling adversary. On October 23, he informed FDR that the people and equipment available for Italy and Overlord were insufficient for "the tasks assigned to them," and that it was preferable to combine resources in the existing operation rather than the prospective one. His position was that the invasion timeline agreed upon at Quebec "should not be interpreted rigidly and without review in the rapidly changing situations of war." Exaggerating the importance of Mediterranean-Aegean operations, he said that success would secure Hitler's eventual defeat, whilst failure would allow him "the chance of a startling comeback."

Seeing the Overlord as a political bribe to Stalin, Churchill told his physician, Lord Moran, 'I will not allow the vast and fruitful campaign in Italy to be squandered away and result in a dreadful disaster, for the sake of crossing the Channel in May.' Unbeknownst to the Americans, he communicated with the Soviet leader a severely negative British report on Allied chances in Italy if extra resources were not committed. An additional personal communication warned that regaining the upper hand in this theater would almost certainly demand the postponing of Overlord. Churchill revealed to Foreign Secretary Anthony Eden, who was tasked with breaking the bad news in Moscow, that "the battle [in Italy] must be nourished until it is fought out and won." We shall do everything we can for OVERLORD, but it is pointless to plan for defeat in the field in order to get brief political satisfaction.'

When Roosevelt and his military advisers learned of Churchill's intrigues, they determined they would no longer accept Churchill's undermining of agreed-upon stances. According to historian David Reynolds, 'OVERLORD was no longer only a strategy; it had become a symbol for who was on top in the Anglo-American alliance.' FDR also received a strong warning about the Soviet thinking on Overlord from America's new envoy in Moscow, Averell Harriman: 'It is hard to overestimate the strategic importance they place on the commencement of the so-called "Second Front" next spring.' As a result, when the three leaders met in Tehran in late November 1943, he decided on a strong demonstration of his support for Stalin's position.

The Soviet leader would go no further for a Big Three summit than Tehran, where he could stay in touch with military actions in Russia via direct telegraph and telephone links with Moscow. Stalin's 'inferiority mentality, whether for himself or for his country,' according to Roosevelt, was the underlying reason for making him go so far, Daisy Suckley wrote in her diary. The trip featured a somewhat pleasant sea passage aboard a US destroyer to Cairo, followed by a long flight from Cairo to Tehran that was guaranteed to be physically demanding, but FDR was certain that the discussion should take place "regardless of the cost to himself."

Churchill's hopes of persuading Roosevelt to support his Mediterranean plan during a pre-Tehran conference in Cairo were dashed. He was unable to speak with the president alone, so he had to make his case at their meeting with the CCS on November 24. He dominated the discussion, blaming missed possibilities in Italy and the Aegean on resource diversion to Overlord. While paying lip respect to the cross-channel promise, he was clearly keen on delaying it, but he was unable to convince the Americans. Later that day, at Roosevelt's request, Harry Hopkins went to see Lord Moran to give the warning, which would soon reach the ears of its intended recipient, that the prime minister should not pursue this approach in the Big Three discussions. 'Sure, we're getting ready for a battle in Tehran,' Hopkins warned. 'You'll see us lined up with the Russians.'

Another conversation between Hopkins and Moran made it plain that Roosevelt was not traveling 8,000 miles to clarify Grand Alliance military strategy, which could have been resolved through the exchange of cables. The trip's goal was to develop a personal relationship with the Soviet leader. According to his emissary, the president is "determined... to come to terms with Stalin, and he will not allow anything to interfere with that purpose." This was consistent with the logic of the Soviet Protocol Committee's assessment of the USSR's expanding might. 'Because Russia is the main force in the fight, she must be given every help and every effort must be made to earn her friendship,' it concluded. Similarly, because she will undoubtedly dominate Europe after the Axis is defeated, it is even more critical to cultivate and preserve the most favorable relations with Russia.

On the second day of the Tehran conference, FDR agreed to transfer his house into the Soviet Embassy as a symbolic show of this intent. The Russian discovery of a German assassination plot made the president's long trek from the American compound to attend meetings at the British and Soviet legations, which were adjacent to each other, unwise. Roosevelt made it easy for them to meet on three occasions without Churchill's presence by accepting Stalin's invitation to host him. On their first meeting, on November 28, he wooed the Soviet leader by exaggerating his differences with the prime minister. In their next meeting, he proposed a postwar world peacekeeping force backed by the political and military might of the 'Four Policemen' - the United States, the Soviet Union, the United Kingdom, and China. Stalin was clearly interested in Roosevelt's idea, despite his misgivings about China's ability to play such a role. Indeed, he desired a more powerful international body than the president had proposed to ensure that a resurrected Germany did not engage in new hostilities. From his position as FDR's interpreter, Charles Bohlen, a Foreign Service officer at the Moscow Embassy, came away with the idea that "Stalin felt it would be much more dangerous to be outside any world organization than to be inside it," as long as the USSR could "block actions it did not like."

In plenary sessions of the Big Three and their top staff, FDR was likewise in lockstep with Stalin on military policy. In the first, he revealed the date for Overlord at Quebec, which the British had refused to share with the Soviets, adding that it should not be delayed by "secondary operations." Stalin therefore advocated that Overlord be "the foundation for all 1944 [Anglo-American] operations" as the most certain way of persuading Hitler to withdraw forces from the eastern front and eventually destroying him. He advised the Anglo-American allies to conduct a parallel landing in the south of France to divert German soldiers away from the English Channel, questioning the prudence of spreading resources to other fronts. This would necessitate the redeployment of all but ten divisions currently fighting in Italy, as well as the postponement of the assault of Rome. FDR requested that the CCS design a plan to attack southern France shortly before, during, or right after the northern invasion. Churchill was left alone in his usual support for Mediterranean-Aegean operations. Later that evening, Lord Moran asked the depressed prime minister whether anything went wrong at the meeting, to which he replied, 'A damned lot has gone wrong.' In contrast, for a buoyant FDR, much had gone right: not only had he shown to Stalin his devotion to the Overlord, but he had also secured guarantees from the Soviet Union that the Soviet Union would enter the war against Japan after Germany was beaten.

The following day's plenary session was much more agonizing for Churchill. Stalin was astounded to learn that no one had yet been appointed to command the Overlord, a strong indication that his friends were not serious about the mission. He insisted on making the appointment in Tehran or as soon as possible following. FDR used the occasion to reiterate that this could only be done after Overlord's priority was fully decided upon.

Instead of committing to this, Churchill digressed into extolling the chances for massive gains in Italy, the Balkans, and the Aegean, even if the investment of resources required to achieve them would demand some delay to the Overlord. In place of realism, he resorted to grandiloquence, declaring that 'now is the moment to reap the crop if we will pay the tiny price for this reaping'. Roosevelt's unequivocal retort that "any operation that might delay it [Overlord] cannot be considered by us" should have ended further debate, but it did not. On the point of losing his cool, Stalin finally addressed Churchill a 'indiscreet question, namely, do the British genuinely believe in Overlord, or are they merely saying so to reassure the Russians?' To avoid a direct response, the prime minister said that if the "conditions" were appropriate, namely that operations in Italy and the Aegean hindered Germany's ability to reinforce its divisions in France, "it was the duty of the British government to hurl every scrap of strength across the channel."

The meeting concluded with an agreement to bring the topic to the Anglo-American CCS to hammer out a consensus position. Stalin was visibly puzzled as to why the Big Three could not address the situation immediately, but the delay allowed FDR to dispatch Hopkins on another private mission. Following a Soviet-hosted evening meal with enormous amounts of food and booze, the aide paid Churchill a late-night visit to make it plain that he was fighting a losing struggle against US-Russian unity on Overlord. The main point was to 'yield with grace.' The following day, the prime minister formally agreed to CCS recommendations that the US and Britain launch Overlord, along with a supporting operation in southern France, 'during May,' with the goal of advancing to the Pisa-Rimini line in the Italian theater by then. Stalin, for his part, restated his determination to coordinate Red Army offensives with Overlord in order to prevent German forces from being diverted from the eastern front.

If the summit had stopped there, FDR's engagement with Stalin would have been an unquestionable success, but their differences on Eastern Europe became clear on the final day. FDR signaled personal acceptance of a Soviet sphere of influence in their final private meeting, while attempting in vain to educate Stalin on American home views. He also agreed that the USSR could keep the territory it had acquired through invasion in 1939 in exchange for Poland obtaining German territory as restitution, a deal he insisted on keeping secret out of fear of losing the Polish-American vote if he ran for a fourth term. Despite appearing to accept this informal commitment, Stalin opposed Anglo-American pressure in the last plenary conference to negotiate a territorial solution with Poland's government-in-exile in London, which he considered anti-Soviet. The Baltic republics of Estonia, Latvia, and Lithuania, which were annexed by the Soviet Union in June 1940, sparked debate in this forum as well. While ready to yield Russian control, FDR wanted them to have some degree of self-determination in line with American public expectations, which clashed with Stalin's insistence on their continued existence as Soviet Socialist Republics.

Tehran bolstered the Grand Alliance's military unity in pursuit of victory against Germany and Japan, while leaving the postwar settlement's political arrangements unsolved. The conference communiqué was signed 'Roosevelt, Stalin, Churchill,' at Stalin's request, reflecting their changing importance on the world stage. This obligated the Allies to seek a "peace that will command the good will of the overwhelming majority of the world's people and banish the scourge and terror of war for many generations," as well as to bring together all nations committed to eradicating "tyranny and slavery, oppression and intolerance... into a world family of democratic nations." This was Roosevelt's personal vision of the future, but he had no illusions that it would be realized anytime soon. For him, the declaration contained a set of goals that the victorious could begin pursuing in peacetime. 'Sometimes I feel that the world will be mighty happy if it obtains 50% of what it seeks out of the war as a lasting success,' he told columnist Walter Lippmann before leaving for Tehran. That may be considered a high average.'

FDR resolved an issue important to keeping Stalin's belief in the Anglo-American commitment to the Overlord at the second Anglo-American conference in Cairo, held on the way back from Tehran. The operation was widely expected to be led by George Marshall, who had the support of Churchill, Stalin, Harry Hopkins, and Henry Stimson, but it was actually led by Dwight Eisenhower. John Pershing, the now-retired commander of US forces in France during World War I, had written to FDR in September, urging that Marshall's 'superior strategical talent and experience' made him irreplaceable in his current position as Army Chief of Staff. The president received the same message from Marshall's JCS colleagues. Roosevelt was well aware that whomever commanded Overlord would be forever remembered if successful. On his way to Tehran, the president stopped in Tunis to meet with Eisenhower, Marshall's potential replacement in the Joint Chiefs of Staff. Observing that field commanders, rather than staff officers, were remembered in popular memory of war, he made the following observation: 'You and I know the name of the Chief of Staff in the Civil War [Henry Halleck], but few Americans outside the professional military do.' FDR managed to console Marshall over a private lunch on 5 December when he informed him of the decision: 'I could not sleep at night with you out of the nation.'

There were good reasons, not just default ones, for handing Eisenhower command. A superb organizer, he had experience of setting up a functioning Allied headquarters for the North Africa-Mediterranean theater, which became the model for the Supreme Headquarters, Allied Expeditionary Force, established in London in January 1944; he was skilled in managing the fractious relations between h He was also a known quantity to Roosevelt, who had assessed him in person in Casablanca and Tunis. When asked by his son, James, why he chose Eisenhower as Overlord commander, FDR replied, "Eisenhower is the best politician among military men." He is a natural leader who can persuade other guys to follow him, which is more important than any other quality in his position.' The appointment, the most important of Roosevelt's presidency, was a huge success, putting Eisenhower on the path to the White House. As both a soldier and a president, he demonstrated highly effective hidden-hand leadership - he didn't worry if other actors thought they were the starting agents as long as he got what he wanted done and in the way he wanted.

Roosevelt did not make Eisenhower's appointment public until he held a Fireside Chat on December 24. Much of his speech concentrated on what kind of world will emerge as a result of the war. In his report on the Tehran summit, he voiced optimism that after Germany and Japan were destroyed, America, Britain, and Russia would be unified in their commitment to eliminate the evil of Nazism and work together for international peace, security, and prosperity. He spoke well of Stalin, promising his audience that "we are going to get along very well with him and the Russian people - very well indeed." His message was clear: America should not retreat to isolationism after the war, lest fresh aggressors undermine the peace. In an apparent reference to the 1930s neutrality laws, he stated,

Former years' well-intended but ill-fated experiments failed. My hope is that we won't try them again. No, it is an overstatement; it is my desire as President and Commander-in-Chief to do everything in my power to ensure that these awful blunders do not happen again. If we are willing to battle for peace now, isn't it reasonable to expect that we will use force to protect the peace in the future?

Regardless of how much Roosevelt tried to focus on peace, the imperative to win the war as soon as possible demanded his attention in 1944. The Allies got bogged down on the Anzio beachhead in late January, an amphibious operation personally designed by Churchill to circumvent German forces in central Italy and conquer Rome. His aspirations for a quick victory were dashed by Anglo-American intelligence underestimating German strength in the area, which fostered erroneous optimism that two infantry divisions without armored backup would suffice for the operation. Anzio, which resembled another Gallipoli, provided Churchill with what he admitted was his darkest moment of the war. As losses on the beach mounted, he told Eisenhower and Alan Brooke in late February, "We hoped to land a wildcat that would tear out the bowels of the Boche." Instead, we've stranded a massive whale, its tail flapping in the water.' He requested another meeting with FDR in vain, hoping for more forces to bail out the company. Roosevelt dissuaded him by claiming bad health - he had been suffering from influenza and bronchitis since late December - and emphasizing his adamant unwillingness to keep Overlord's landing craft in the Mediterranean.

When the Allies ultimately broke out of Anzio in late May, US General Mark Clark marched towards Rome rather than entrapping the German 10th Army as ordered. His arrival in the city on June 4th did nothing to bring the conflict to an end because German soldiers had merely moved northward to a new defensive line. FDR acknowledged the symbolic significance of Rome being the first Axis capital to fall in a Fireside Chat to commemorate this victory, but advised the people not to exaggerate its military significance. 'Victory,' he declared,'still remains some distance ahead... it will be challenging and costly, as I have told you many, many times.'

As FDR was well aware, the invasion of France was a necessary prelude to the Third Reich's demise. In late January, Anglo-

American military strategists decided to postpone D-Day by a month in order to assure sufficient ships and landing craft for the biggest amphibious assault in history. Storms in the English Channel forced a 24-hour postponement of the scheduled date of June 5. Eisenhower's decision to use a brief period of improved weather to authorize an invasion on 6 June was the most significant of his leadership. Nonetheless, he had already demonstrated confident and persuasive leadership, fulfilling FDR's faith in him. He insisted on having subordinate commanders he knew and trusted for Overlord, even if it meant depleting the Mediterranean theater. Under threat of resigning, he persuaded Anglo-American air commanders to divert bombers from the aerial war over Germany to the 'transportation plan,' which involved cutting off rail and road communications in northern France months before the invasion to isolate the area where it would take place. He also insisted on the Anvil invasion of southern France in support of Overlord, despite Churchill's threat to resign over the diversion of resources away from the Italian campaign.

Despite British reservations about Overlord's chances, the invasion was actually a collaborative effort. Americans were utterly committed to the mission, and they were willing to launch the initial assault with only a slim margin of Allied ground-force superiority to take the beaches before pouring in significantly more troops and machines for a breakout from the coastal perimeter. General Sir Frederick Morgan, Chief of Staff to the Supreme Allied Commander and a crucial figure in invasion planning, subsequently said, 'I believe it is a little exaggeration to suggest that the total enormity of Overlord was not realized by some of the British higher-ups until quite late in the day.' Nonetheless, the decision to land in Normandy rather than Pas de Calais, which offered the shortest passage and most direct route into Germany, as well as the deception strategy to divert German attention to the latter, were entirely British in idea.

By the evening of the first day of the invasion, Allied troops had battled their way inland from the Normandy shore, establishing five non-contiguous beachheads ranging along a 60-mile line. At 8.30

p.m. EST, FDR appeared on the radio and asked the nation to join him in prayer for all involved in this "mighty endeavor." His words, somber and solemn, expressed a fatalistic resignation reminiscent of Abraham Lincoln's Civil War oratory about the necessity of battle on this scale to destroy "the unholy forces of our enemy" and build a "peace that will let all of men live in freedom, reaping the just rewards of their honest toil." The effort appeared to have convinced Stalin that his Anglo-American allies were now reliable allies in the struggle against Hitler. He told Averell Harriman that the amphibious operation was "an unheard of achievement, the magnitude of which had never been undertaken in the history of warfare."

The Allies ultimately pushed through the coastal zone in late July and liberated Paris on the 24th and 25th of August. Meanwhile, the Soviet Bagration onslaught into Byelorussia destroyed twenty divisions of Hitler's Army Group Centre and advanced 450 kilometers in five weeks, beginning on June 22. This was Germany's most humiliating defeat during the war. Regardless of future setbacks, the Grand Alliance was definitely on its way to defeating Hitler. FDR delegated responsibility for the last stages of the war in Europe to his military officers in Washington and Eisenhower. His health problems had been far worse than acknowledged to the public since his return from Tehran. In his final year, he worked just four hours a day, often less, and required frequent breaks away from the White House. As his energies faded, FDR engaged with fewer commander-in-chief responsibilities in order to focus on establishing a lasting peace.

Nonetheless, Roosevelt felt obligated to intervene personally in a debate about the bi-axial approach undertaken against Japan. Admiral Chester Nimitz, commander of the Pacific Ocean Areas, dealt another crushing defeat to the Imperial Navy in the Battle of the Philippine Sea on 19-20 June 1944, opening the Marianas to amphibious invasion, the success of which would place Japan within range of new B-29 bombers. As commander of the Southwest Pacific, General Douglas MacArthur focused on acquiring control of the northern coast of New Guinea, from which he could launch an attack on the Philippines. Each commander, certain that his unique policy gave the best chance of victory in the Pacific, demanded vast more resources to pursue it. To mediate between them, FDR conducted a cross-country train excursion from Washington DC to San Diego, then boarded the USS Baltimore for a meeting with MacArthur and Nimitz in Hawaii.

Surprisingly, the day after his arrival on July 26, Roosevelt directed his two commanders to accompany him in the back of an open-top limousine for a six-hour assessment of military installations on Oahu. This was the commander-in-chief's third visit to an active theater of war in eighteen months, following stops in North Africa and Sicily on his way home from Tehran. The visit provided excellent opportunities for press photography and film footage of America's revival in the Pacific. This required more activity than FDR had done in a single day since Tehran, yet he managed to pull off one last surprise. Nimitz and MacArthur were expecting to give their strategic speeches the next day, but they were called to do so after dinner on the second evening. Admiral William Leahy, the president's only JCS member on this tour, praised the president's chairing of this session. 'Roosevelt was at his best as he deftly led the conversation from one point to the next and limited the area of difference between MacArthur and Nimitz,' he wrote. The entire discussion was conducted in a really nice manner.'

Deferring a final decision until the next day, FDR had no trouble convincing both commanders to accept a compromise that provided each portion of what he desired. Although the Honolulu meeting effectively continued the bi-axial method, it took the sting out of the Nimitz-MacArthur rivalry, provided the two theater commanders a better understanding of each other's ideas, and helped them work better together. After completing the Marianas campaign successfully in November, Nimitz began constructing airfields on the island chain in preparation for the air assault on the Japanese mainland and the invasion of Iwo Jima and Okinawa in 1945. Meanwhile, MacArthur got all available naval help to begin retaking the Philippine islands, an operation that would deny the Imperial Navy a base from which to assault Nimitz's advance plan.

FDR's swansong as commander-in-chief was the Hawaii conference, but he consented to Churchill's request for an utterly superfluous Anglo-American summit in Quebec in mid-September 1944. Shocked by his haggard appearance, British attendees were concerned that his hesitant and disengaged demeanor at plenary meetings indicated deterioration of mental powers. Nonetheless, FDR was capable of dismissing Churchill's efforts to redefine Allied strategy. To the chagrin of his own colleagues, the prime minister recommended that once German forces were driven out of Italy, Anglo-American forces should advance over the Adriatic to Trieste and then move north, aiming to reach Vienna before the Red Army. FDR's courteous but effective response advised against underestimating the Germans' ability and willingness to battle on. The priority, he argued, was crossing the Rhine, which he described as "a formidable obstacle," before embarking on the massive job of conquering the Wehrmacht in its heartland. With Hitler's final onslaught, the close-run fight of the Bulge, barely three months away, Roosevelt foresaw that 'the Germans could not yet be counted out, and one more huge fight would have to be fought.' Churchill also failed with another suggestion for the Allies to focus their efforts in the fight against Japan on recapturing Singapore, a clear attempt to co-opt US might in recreating the British empire in Asia. FDR flatly refused to risk significant fatalities with a direct attack on a heavily fortified enemy position. In his final year of life, when failing health required him to achieve a daily balance between leisure and labor, Roosevelt was no longer the leader of old. With victory in the war now a question of time, he primarily delegated authority to his military commanders and focused on establishing a lasting peace. Until early 1944, he was a very effective and engaged commander-in-chief, meeting the challenges of economic mobilization, command organization, strategic leadership, and alliance-building with considerable success. He took America to the brink of triumph in two epic wars fought simultaneously on opposite sides of the globe, while incurring only 2% of total casualties. 'Of the big individuals at the top [during the Second World War], Roosevelt was the only one who knew what he was doing: he made the United States the greatest force in the world at essentially no expense,' historian A. J. P. Taylor says. This scathing remark, although underestimating FDR's national-security goals, held more than a grain of truth. The United States emerged from the war with half the world's manufacturing capacity, two-thirds of the world's gold reserves, three-quarters of the world's investment capital, the world's largest navy and air force, and the world's first atomic armament. Roosevelt was essential in developing his country into a powerhouse, and in doing so, he turned the president from a national to a worldwide office.

10

Practical visionary

FDR's national-security presidency

The concept of security was crucial to Franklin D. Roosevelt's presidency. He had established himself as the first economic-security president through New Deal initiatives to safeguard Americans from the miseries of the Great Depression. In the late 1930s, in response to Germany, Italy, and Japan's escalating bellicosity, he became the first national-security president. FDR pioneered the concept of national security, which had hitherto been an inconsequential term in American political jargon, to warn his fellow citizens that these hostile powers jeopardized not just their nation's borders but also its essential values. He promulgated a new strategic doctrine that affected American foreign policy into the twenty-first century by moving beyond the customary emphasis on defense from attack to place equal importance on defense of America's belief-system. 'Until FDR,' historian Andrew Preston observed, 'no American president had presented security as having two equal pieces - physical and normative, territorial and ideological - constituting an integrated, indivisible whole that applied the globe over.'

As president during the war, FDR desired a peace solution that would assure America's postwar national security. To him, the only way to create an external environment that did not jeopardize US interests and values was to ensure that they were shared by as many countries as possible. As a result, he envisioned a new world order founded on the liberties reflected by self-determination, increased living standards, and peaceful coexistence. Meanwhile, once peace was restored, Roosevelt sought to strengthen domestic economic stability through New Deal development. In his opinion that democracy's well-being in America supported its spread abroad, both types of security were essentially interrelated. Even if he had to moderate his idealistic ideas of national security and economic security with compromises that yielded contradicting realities in actuality, they remained the guiding lights for his wartime thinking. In his belief that good politics could achieve great things, realism and idealism were not mutually exclusive. According to historian Warren Kimble, 'Franklin Roosevelt was no ideologue, but he had an ideology.'

Before America went to war, FDR's thinking on a national-security peace had progressed to an advanced point. One of his best speeches, the 1941 State of the Union Address, cited the Four Freedoms to support the implementation of the Lend-Lease policy. He declared that this was a "moment unprecedented in the history of the Union...because at no previous time has American security been as seriously threatened from without as it is today." It was his responsibility to declare that 'the future and safety of our country and democracy are overwhelmingly implicated in events far beyond our borders'. FDR said that arming individuals who were resisting aggressors "strengthens the... security of our nation," but there was far more at issue than territorial defense.

According to Roosevelt, the strength of America's democracy was determined by its ability to provide certain public goods, including equality of opportunity, jobs for everyone who wanted to work, social assistance, the elimination of special privilege, the preservation of civil liberties, and a rising standard of living. 'Many problems related to our social economy require quick adjustment,' he admitted. Because the ending sentence determined the address's meaning in history, this implied demand for New Deal growth would fade from memory. Until this point, presidential speechwriters had mostly written the discourse, but FDR wrote it himself. It envisioned a "world founded on four essential freedoms": free speech and expression, religious freedom, freedom from want, and freedom from fear. Following the invocation of each freedom, the words 'anywhere in the world' were added. 'That covers an awful lot of territory, Mr. President,' said Harry Hopkins, who was skeptical of their inclusion. I'm not sure how interested Americans will be in the people of Java.' 'I'm afraid they'll have to be some day, Harry,' said FDR, unfazed. The world is shrinking to the point where folks in Java are becoming our neighbors.'

The term remained in the speech to represent Roosevelt's vision of a moral world order based on "the cooperation of free countries, working together in a friendly, civilized society," rather than the dictators' desire for a "new order of tyranny." In FDR's thinking, the invocation of the Four Freedoms as a worldwide ideal supplemented the New Deal's interpretation of freedom at home. He blamed fascist aggressiveness on an unregulated worldwide economy, blaming unrestricted capitalism for the Great Depression. If the solution to the domestic issue resided in the state's assurance of economic security, it followed that restoring global peace and stability would necessitate a rules-based world order backed by multilateral institutions.

Roosevelt did not create his concept of national security in a vacuum. The concept gained traction in the late 1930s among geopolitics academics at major colleges, including Princeton's Edward Mead Earle, Yale's Nicolas Spykman, and Johns Hopkins' Albert Weinberg. It also had supporters among national thinking leaders, most notably Walter Lippmann. America's most prominent columnist commented in 1944, perfectly expressing the concept. This continuous propagation of Americanism in the outside world must reflect more than self-righteousness. Yes, it does. It represents the fact that no nation, and definitely not our nation, can survive in a politically alien and morally unfriendly environment, as well as the profound and enduring truth that a people who does not advance their faith has already begun to relinquish it.

At the Atlantic Conference, held from August 9 to 12, 1941, aboard ships (the US Navy cruiser Augusta and the Royal Navy battleship Prince of Wales) in Placentia Bay, off the coast of Newfoundland, FDR elevated such ideas into international policy. According to Harry Hopkins, 'they established an easy intimacy, a laughing informality, and a moratorium on pomposity and cant - and also a degree of frankness which, if not quite total, was astonishingly close to it.' On August 10, their meeting served as a symbolic statement of similar beliefs during the Sunday service aboard the Prince of Wales. The emotional impact of the hymn-singing led Churchill to openly cry. 'If nothing else had happened while we were here, that would have cemented us,' FDR told his son Elliott.Onward, Christian Soldiers." We are, and with God's aid, we will continue.'

Despite America's neutrality, Roosevelt and Churchill reached an agreement on a unified declaration of war intentions, which was delivered as a radio cable for press publication. This 376-word document became known as the Atlantic Charter, a phrase invented by the Daily Herald, the newspaper of the British Labour Party. The two leaders had ultimate say over the contents, which were meticulously drafted by Under Secretary of State Sumner Welles and Permanent Undersecretary for Foreign Affairs Sir Alexander Cadogan. Though not legally signed, the statement's non-parchment form anticipated the current summitry's dependence on media to communicate its successes.In its final form, the Atlantic Charter embodied American liberalism's worldview. It outlined eight universal principles for a "better future for the world." First, America and Britain disavowed aggrandizement ambition; second, both opposed territorial changes against the wishes of peoples affected; third, each respected 'the right of all peoples to choose the form of government under which they will live' and promised restoration of self-government to those forcibly deprived of it by war; fourth, they aspired to ensure equal access for all nations to trade and raw materials required for prosperity; and fifth, they sought to ensure equal access for all nations to trade and raw materials The sixth principle said that both countries desired a peace that provided all nations with "the means of dwelling within their own boundaries, and... assurance that all the men in all the lands may live out their lives free from fear and want." The final obligation was to protect the freedom of the seas. Finally, America and Britain understood that all nations' "abandonment of the use of force" required aggressors to disarm "pending the establishment of a larger and permanent system of general security."

The Big Three alliance swiftly disintegrated without Roosevelt to hold it together. The advent of the Cold War took on an appearance of inevitability as it developed over its more than four-decade existence. One of the most intriguing 'what-if' puzzles is whether history would have turned out differently if FDR had lived longer. Churchill's wartime foreign secretary was among those who had no reservations. Anthony Eden criticized the turn toward Cold War conflict in an August 1946 confidential discussion with Robert Sherwood, which was barred from inclusion in his memoir of FDR's wartime partnership with Harry Hopkins. Roosevelt, he asserted, "would never have allowed the current situation to develop," and his death was "a calamity of immeasurable proportions."86 Anticipating a lengthy transition to an international system that resembled his national-security vision, Roosevelt's grand strategy for laying the groundwork for its development was to build a Great Power peace, maintain Stalin's trust, and avoid becoming distracted into confrontation on issues unrelated to his ultimate goal.

Printed in Great Britain
by Amazon

45162118R00086